JANE'S POCKET BOOK OF SUBMARINE DEVELOPMENT

Edited by John E. Moore

MACDONALD AND JANE'S

FIRST PUBLISHED 1976

COPYRIGHT © JOHN E. MOORE 1976

ISBN 0356 04799 7 (PVC EDITION)
ISBN 0356 04798 9 (LIBRARY EDITION)

This edition is not available for sale in the United States, its dependencies,
the Philippine Islands or the Dominion of Canada.

PUBLISHED BY MACDONALD AND JANE'S PUBLISHERS LTD
PAULTON HOUSE, 8 SHEPHERDESS WALK, LONDON N1 7LW

FOREWORD

During the seventy-five years since submarines became operational their true function has been very largely misunderstood by both the general public and the naval staffs of the fleets to which they belonged. As a result both good ideas and valuable innovations have been wasted and wild schemes and designs promoted. Since 1901 the home of British submarines, HMS *Dolphin*, has had as its motto *"Venio non videor"* – "I come unseen". It is this very attribute which is too often forgotten and the submarine has frequently been regarded as a surface vessel with a capability to dive – should this be required. The majority of the pioneers realised the error of this viewpoint and aimed at a boat which would be on the surface only when the limitations of its propulsion machinery so dictated. In the earlier days the prime limitation was lack of battery power which kept the dived endurance down and reduced the operational speed. As a result, the submarine was forced to the surface for passage to and from the patrol area and to charge her batteries when there. During these periods of visibility she was the prey to both ships and aircraft. The aim of the designers should therefore have been the increase of underwater speed and endurance, yet this most necessary advance was held up by the pursuit of totally fallacious theories of submarine warfare and the boats that were their outcome. The means of achieving this aim were, from time to time, available but were only too frequently ignored. In 1915 the British "R" class was designed for an underwater speed of 15 knots, unheard of until then, but this class was succeeded by the monsters of the "K" class, steam-driven boats designed to operate with the fleet, diving only at the last minute. So a submarine could move faster under water and needed only the ability to charge its batteries whilst dived. Thus one would have thought that the invention of the Schnorkel-mast, providing an efficient and sufficient intake of air whilst still submerged, would have been greeted with delight. But, when offered to the British in 1938, it was turned down and it was only after the successful use of it by the Germans had been proved that the Royal Navy adopted the snort after the Second World War. The number of valuable lives and submarines which would have been saved is incalculable but must certainly have been considerable, whilst efficiency would have been greatly increased by doing away with the need to withdraw from a focal area to surface and charge.

Thus the submariner at sea was put at an unnecessary disadvantage for many years and it is the aim of this book to describe the slow, and sometimes faltering, advance of this particular type of warship. There are many ways in which it could have been done. Here the main submarine-operating countries (France, Italy, Japan, the UK, USA and USSR) have been chosen, as it has been from their yards and drawing-boards that the main bulk of the world's submarines have come. Other navies, notably those of Netherlands and Sweden, have designed and built their own classes but it is from a choice of classes from the main building countries that the submarine's evolution can best be traced. In the same way that some countries have had to be left out, so some classes have also been omitted. I can only apologise to my many submariner friends if they fail to find their own country or their favourite boat listed. They, above all others, will appreciate the problems set by lack of space.

The origin of the submarine is somewhat confused by myth and legend. Alexander the Great in his diving bell, designs by Leonardo da Vinci are of little practical value since they led to nothing. Even the accurate and efficient hypotheses of William

Bourne in 1578 failed to provide his "submersible boat" with any form of propulsion although he described a "breathing tube" which was a near ancester of today's snort mast. Van Drebbel, a Dutchman living in England, adopted Bourne's theories and produced a pair of boats capable of submersion, being propelled by oars when dived.

Although King James I showed interest, no further action appears to have been taken in England and it was in Holland in 1653 that the Frenchman de Son built a submersible catamaran with a clockwork-driven paddle-wheel between the hulls. Unfortunately the spring was not up to the job and this lack of a means of propulsion was probably the main inhibition in submarine design for the next century.

Despite further attempts in England it was the American David Bushnell who produced the first submersible craft which had any possibility of being used in war – the one-man crank-operated *Turtle*. Ezra Lee is a famous name in submarines being that of the first man to make contact with an enemy warship from under water. Through lack of an efficient means of securing the weapon this attack (September 6th, 1776) on Lord Hawke's flagship off New York failed. Had it been successful and been followed by others the course, though not the outcome, of the War of Independence might have been altered.

No success, therefore, attended Bushnell's efforts and it was more than twenty years until another American, Robert Fulton, produced plans for a submarine craft called *Nautilus*. He was the first man to conceive the role of the submarine as a deterrent to war, believing its capabilities such that, if built in sufficient numbers, all surface warships could be sunk. Being a revolutionary in both thought and action, Fulton offered his ideas to the French to ensure

the defeat of the British Navy. His price was high and the plan was rejected by the Directory. After an unsuccessful visit to Holland Fulton found a sympathetic reception at Napoleon's new court. In 1800 *Nautilus* was completed, some twenty-five feet long, hand propelled with a crew of three. To ease their efforts a sail was provided for passage but, despite this 9-ton boat being a great advance on the *Turtle,* no solution was provided to the weapon problem. All *Nautilus* had was a large spike to be forced into the target's hull, thus attaching a floating charge with a contact fuse. This was intended to explode on striking the target's hull but there are only two reports of its success – against an old ship in a demonstration in 1801 and in a similar trial off Walmer in 1805. This evidence resulted in the too frequent reaction of naval staffs to what is original innovation – rejection. In 1804 Fulton came to terms with his conscience and offered his ideas to the British – despite Pitt's encouragement rejection was again the result. Lord St. Vincent, with a mixture of reactionary approach and remarkable foresight, gave his well-known verdict to Fulton – that this was "a mode of warfare which those who commanded the seas did not want and which, if successful, would deprive them of it." Success was to depend on the two things which submariners have been seeking during the last hundred years – efficient and economical propulsion and a competent weapon system.

Nearly half a century later, in 1850, a new name entered submarine history, Wilhelm Bauer. His craft, *Der Brandtaucher,* was a slab-sided vessel, a little bigger than *Nautilus,* and built of sheet-iron. Neither the propulsion, a hand-driven screw, nor the weapon, a species of mine, showed any improvement on those of her predecessor. But Bauer had appreciated a problem known only too well to trimming-officers of succeeding generations: that of maintaining the submarine horizontal when dived. His solution was a simple fore-and-aft screw carrying a heavy weight which was moved as necessary to alter the trim. In February 1851, whilst the boat was on trials off Kiel, she gained depth until the flat-sided hull was crushed and she settled on the bottom. Bauer appreciated yet another submarine problem, that of free escape. Having calmed his crew of two, he flooded the craft, equalised the pressure and then released the hatch, subsequently making the first free ascent in history.

This disaster caused a loss of German interest and Bauer, after discussions with the Austrians, joined forces with the Russians. Under the patronage of the Grand Duke Constantine he built *Le Diable-Marin* of 52 feet and with a beam of 12 feet, capable of diving to 100 feet. A diver's lock was provided to allow the exit and re-entry of a diver who was to attach charges to the target's hull. Bauer had anticipated the X-craft of 1943. Despite successful trials by *Le Diable-Marin* the Russians, occupied with the Crimean War, were less than enthusiastic. Although, after the loss of the first boat, they invited Bauer to try again, he was equally unenthusiastic about his hosts. Despite an encouraging visit to France in 1858 he had built his last submarine and died seventeen years later in Germany. Had he found any imaginative support this brilliant and devoted man could well have advanced the programme of submarine evolution by many years.

Once again it was from America, from the Confederate States of the Civil War, that new advances were to come. Under the stress of the Northern blockade the *Davids* were produced. The first of these, built in 1863, were barely eligible for the term "submarine", as at no time were they designed for total submergence. These were the first boats which relied on the sea to screen the majority of their hulls and they were to be propelled by steam. This necessitated keeping a low casing, a hatch and the funnel above water. These protrusions above the surface, when added to their weapon, a spar carrying a 130lb charge, made them extremely vulnerable in the event of a successful attack. In the only one recorded, on the *Ironsides* on October 5th, 1863, the target was damaged, but the *David* sank after the backwash of the explosion flooded through the open hatch.

Realising this peril a new design was produced by Horace L. Hunley in mid 1863. This type reverted to hand propulsion by eight men and was conned through ports in the short "conning tower". She was capable of total submergence for a couple of hours and, although fitted with hydroplanes aft, must have been a pig to handle. She was over sixty feet long and only four feet in the beam and it was this which caused her instability. She plunged in the mud on trials, but was salved. On February 17th, 1864 a new crew carried out the first fully successful dived attack on a surface ship, the 1300-ton steam sloop *Housatonic*. The target was sunk but so also was the attacker.

The last of the *Davids*, another semi-submerging craft, was produced in 1864. She was a conversion from a small patrol-craft which, fitted with ballast tanks, trimmed down for the final approach, again using the lethal spar-charge.

These were desperate measures in a navy in a parlous situation. In France, however, ingenious plans were laid to provide her navy with advances unknown to her rivals. In 1858 *La Gloire*, the world's first ironclad, was launched and the same year the plans of Capitaine de Vaisseau Bourgois were put out to tender. These were for a large submarine propelled by compressed air and the ensuing competition was won by the designs of M. de Brun. His craft, *Le Plongeur,* was launched at Rochefort in 1863 and ran trials two years later. For her time she was a mammoth, being 140 feet long with a displacement of 410 tons. Apart from her size *Le Plongeur's* main interest lies in her propulsion and ballast tanks. The former was achieved by a four cylinder engine driven by compressed air which was stored in large cylinders throughout the boat. For the first time this air was used for blowing main ballast. Despite these advances *Le Plongeur's* armament was still a charge on the end of a spar, and this lack of a satisfactory weapon, added to the submarine's highly eccentric depth-keeping, caused the French Navy to abandon the trials. The problem of trim was far from solution and anyone who has experienced a submarine porpoising before the trim is effectively caught must feel great sympathy for these pioneers.

Whilst France was embroiled in the war with Prussia and its aftermath others were entering the submarine field. At the head of the Adriatic the search for a suitable weapon was completed in 1866. Robert Whitehead, an Englishman managing an engineering company at Fiume designed and built the first satisfactory torpedo, named after a member of the ray family of fishes armed with organs in the head designed to give an electric shock. By 1872 Whitehead had started his own torpedo factory at Fiume and these weapons soon incorporated the steadying effect of the gyroscope invented by M.L. Obry of Trieste in 1876.

Thus one of the two major problems had been overcome. An original approach to the propulsive problem was made by Reverend G.W. Garrett who adapted the principle of the "fireless locomotive" – a boiler which would continue to give stored heat after the boiler was damped down. His craft, hopefully named *Resurgam,* was a larger edition of a smaller model, and built by Cochranes of Liverpool in 1879. Only 45 feet long she was wrecked during trials but her results were sufficiently good for Thorsten Nordenfelt to adopt the plans for a torpedo-carrying underwater vehicle to be built in Stockholm. This boat of about 60 tons was virtually untrimmable, had insufficient power and speed to obtain much value from her single pair of hydroplanes and adopted strange attitudes when the single torpedo was discharged. Nevertheless Nordenfelt sold one craft to Greece, two to Turkey, one to Russia, which was lost before delivery, and the plans for the unsuccessful W1 and 2 built in Germany in 1890.

These boats must have been sold on the basis of Nordenfelt's enormous reputation for they were behind in their propulsion system and thoroughly unsound in the design of their depth-keeping systems. Frequently depth-keeping relies on speed and speed requires power. This was not to be found in manual, compressed-air or latent heat propulsion. In Russia, from 1876, Drzwiecki produced a series of submarines propelled by pedals – boats primitive in certain aspects but containing the earliest form of periscope and a method of air-purification combining pure oxygen input with the forerunner of today's soda-lime air purifiers. No doubt his cyclists needed the maximum of cleaned and enriched air but they were outdated by contemporary development. Otto's principle of the four-stroke engine was announced in 1876 and Daimler, Diesel and Clerk were applying and improving this in the late 1870s and 1880s. Faraday's electric motor was also now available and it needed little time for these advances to be applied to submarines.

In 1888 Lieutenant Isaac Peral superintended the building of a submarine at Cadiz which was powered by an electric motor. Despite this tremendous advance the Spanish staff, paying more heed to Peral's youth and arrogance than to the inherent advantages of his designs, shelved his plans. In the war with the USA, which started in 1894, some Spaniards may have had the grace to think of the advantages discarded through stiff-necked refusal to look rather at the facts than at the man.

During this period of activity at Cadiz the French had revived their interest in underwater affairs. Claude Goubet produced two manually-operated craft in 1886-89 which had neither adequate propulsion nor suitable weapon. Simultaneously Dupuy de Lôme (architect of *La Gloire*) had turned his attention to submarine design. After his death in 1885 Gustave Zédé continued the work which resulted in the completion of *Gymnote* in 1888. She was a few months behind Peral's boat in having electric propulsion, which was housed in a sheet-steel hull 60 feet long. Her diving performance was later improved by fitting bow and midships hydroplanes and her performance merited the construction of a larger boat, the *Gustave Zédé*. Named after her first designer and completed by Romazzotti she was 160 feet long, electrically propelled, carried three torpedoes and was a brute to handle when dived. Extra hydroplanes were added and her improved performance was reflected in the trials of her successor the *Morse*, who also carried a periscope. But *Morse*'s performance was overshadowed by the appearance of *Narval*, the brain-child of Maxime Laubeuf. As the winner of an international competition in 1896 he placed France in the forefront of submarine affairs with his entry. *Narval* was a double-hull design with a proper casing, hydroplanes both forward and aft and carrying four torpedoes in slings. She was the first boat designed in Europe which had dual propulsion – steam for surface running and an electric motor for dived work. The boiler was oil fired with the fuel stored in the tanks of the double hull and *Narval* had the capability to recharge her batteries from a generator driven by the main steam-engine. Two periscopes were fitted and, all-in-all, she was probably the greatest single step in submarine design to date. Her commissioning in June 1900 marked the beginning of a long line of successful boats, now leading to the first French nuclear fleet submarine.

While all this activity continued in Europe, joined by Delfino in Italy, across the Atlantic much was happening.

The undoubted leader in this movement was J.P. Holland, an Irishman who emigrated to the USA in 1873, taking with him a hatred of the British and a desire to do them harm. In four years, at the age of 37, he had borrowed $6000 and built *Holland I*. This was smaller than a modern torpedo, 16 feet long and of 20 inches beam, propelled by pedals worked by its single operator in his diving-suit. A year later, in 1878, *Holland II* appeared, a little larger and fitted with an unsatisfacory engine. Her problems were those of so many of her contemporaries – propulsion, weapon and trimming. Nevertheless the Fenian Society were sufficiently impressed to subscribe towards the building of *Holland III*. Wrangles caused a break-up of this partnership and the craft was abandoned. *Holland IV* followed in 1883, only 16 feet long but financed from the meagre resources of the John P. Holland Torpedo Boat Co. She sank alongside and was succeeded by *Holland V*, financed from outside the company. Her armament was a pneumatic gun discharging a dynamite-filled shell. In her trials in 1887 she failed in all ways and Holland was too discouraged to continue. But the USN had set aside a quarter of a million dollars for submarine development and in 1895 announced an open competition, a year before that in France. Holland's entry was selected before those of

Lake, Baker and many others. The staff requirements were over-severe but the contract was signed in 1895 and two years later *Holland VII*, (no record of *Holland VI* is available) named *Plunger*, was launched. In the well-known fashion of some naval staffs, continual changes were made to the staff requirements and, as a result, trials were left uncompleted and Holland embarked on a private venture, *Holland VIII*. Despite financial aid, this effort forced the builder to sell out to the Electric Storage Battery Co. and the famous Electric Boat Co. was thus formed. The boat was only 74 tons but in her "cigar-shaped" hull incorporated an Otto petrol engine of 50hp, an electric motor giving 5 knots dived and mounted a single torpedo tube. She proved safe and handy, looked astonishingly like the 1943 X-craft and in April 1900 the USN bought her for $120,000. The long line of Holland boats which follow in this book had started and it is interesting to find that the Royal Navy's Submarine Service was founded on the product of such a violently anti-British inventor. Despite the excellent designs of Simon Lake, he failed to understand the true principles of submarine operations and though his name appears frequently in these pages it was Holland who had made the greatest advance in the evolution of the submarine.

ACKNOWLEDGEMENTS

The editor and publishers wish to thank all those who have provided photographs and drawings for this book. In particular, we would like to thank the following for their help: Samuel Morrison, Norman Polmar, Albert Pavia, Raymond Blackman, Antony Preston and Anthony Watts. Special acknowledgement is also due to the Royal Navy, ECP Armées, the US Navy and Wright & Logan.

U.S.A.

Type: Holland VIII
Class: "Plunger II"
Displacement, tons: 74
Dimensions, feet: 54 x 10.7 x 10.5
Torpedo Armament: 3 torpedoes
Guns: Originally fitted with dynamite gun
Main machinery: 4-cylinder petrol engine; 50hp

Speed, knots: 8 surfaced; 5 dived
Dates: 1896
Special features: 1,050 gallons petrol carried

Notes: The USS *Holland* was the first submarine of the US Navy and was accepted in 1900.

Holland (U.S. Navy)

U.S.A.

Type: Holland IX (7)
Class: "Adder"
Displacement, tons: 120
Dimensions, feet: 63.5 x 11.7 x 12
Torpedo armament: 1 torpedo tube; 5 x 18in torpedoes
Main machinery: Petrol engine/Electric motor; 160hp
Speed, knots: 9 surfaced; 7 dived

Complement: 7
Dates: 1896-1902
Special features: 850 gallons petrol carried. Range 800 miles at 9 knots

Notes: *Adder, Grampus, Moccasin, Pike, Plunger, Porpoise, Shark*. Later A1-A7.

Plunger (U.S. Navy)

U.S.A.

Type: Holland (3)
Class: "Cuttlefish"
Displacement, tons: 170
Dimensions, feet: 81
Torpedo armament: 1 torpedo tube
Main machinery: Petrol engine

Speed, knots: 10 surfaced; 8 dived
Dates: 1906-1907
Special features: Range 500 miles at 9 knots. 2 periscopes

Notes: *Cuttlefish, Viper, Tarantula.* Later B1-B3.

Tarantula (U.S. Navy)

U.S.A.

Type: Holland (5)
Class: "Octopus"
Displacement, tons: 238 surfaced; 275 dived
Dimensions, feet: ? x ? x 14.7
Torpedo armament: 2 torpedo tubes
Main machinery: Petrol engine; 500hp
Speed, knots: 11 surfaced; 10 dived

Complement: 10
Dates: 1907-1909
Special features: Range 900 miles at 9 knots surfaced; 80 at 5 knots dived

Notes: *Octopus*-C1, *Stingray*-C2, *Tarpon*-C3, *Bonita*-C4, *Snapper*-C5.

Snapper (U.S. Navy)

U.S.A.

Type: Holland (3)
Class: "Narwhal"
Displacement, tons: 280 surfaced; 345 dived
Dimensions, feet: 134.5 x 14 x 14.7
Torpedo armament: 2 torpedo tubes
Main machinery: Petrol engine; 600hp

Speed, knots: 13 surfaced; 9 dived
Complement: 15
Dates: 1909

Notes: *Narwhal, Grayling, Salmon.* Later D1-D3.

Narwhal (U.S. Navy)

U.S.A.

Type: Holland (7)
Class: "Skipjack" (later E1-3 & F1-4)
Displacement, tons: 350 surfaced; 435 dived
Torpedo armament: 2 torpedo tubes
Main machinery: Petrol
Speed, knots: 14 surfaced; 11 dived
Complement: 15

Dates: 1910-1911
Special features: Range 2,500 miles at 11 knots surfaced, 100 at 5 knots dived

Notes: *Skipjack, Barracuda, Carp, Pickerel, Skate, Sturgeon, Tuna.* Later E1-3 and F1-4.

Sturgeon (U.S. Navy)

U.S.A.

Type: Lake (3)
Class: "G1-G3"
Displacement, tons: 540 dived
Torpedo armament: 6 torpedo tubes
Main machinery: 1,200hp

Speed, knots: 14 surfaced; 10 dived
Dates: 1910-1911

Notes: A "Lake" design which was improved in "G4".

G1

U.S.A.

Type: Laurenti (1)
Class: "G4"
Displacement, tons: 358 surfaced; 458 dived
Dimensions, feet: 157.5 x 17.5 x 16
Torpedo armament: 4 x 18in torpedo tubes
Main machinery: Petrol engine; 1,000hp surfaced, 440hp dived

Speed, knots: 14 surfaced; 9.5 dived
Dates: 1912
Special features: 10 ton drop keel. 12 hours endurance dived

Notes: Previously *Thrasher*.

G4

U.S.A.

Type: Holland (3)
Class: "H1-H3"
Displacement, tons: 430 dived
Dimensions, feet: 150 x 16 x 15
Torpedo armament: 4 x 18in torpedo tubes
Main machinery: Petrol; 800hp
Speed, knots: 14 surfaced; 11 dived

Complement: 25
Dates: 1911-1913
Special features: Range 2,300 miles at 11 knots surfaced, 100 at 5 knots dived

Notes: Previously *Seawolf* (H1), *Nautilus* (H2), *Garfish* (H3). H1 built by Union Iron Works, H3 by Moran and Company.

Garfish (U.S. Navy)

U.S.A.

Type: Holland (8)
Class: "K1-K8"
Displacement, tons: 390 surfaced; 520 dived
Dimensions, feet: 153.5 x 16.7 x 13
Torpedo armament: 4 torpedo tubes (bow); 8 torpedoes carried
Main machinery: 2 sets 6-cylinder; 500bhp surfaced; Nelseco diesels; 2 x 340hp electric motors
Speed, knots: 14.1 surfaced; 10.6 dived
Complement: 28

Dates: 1912-1914
Special features: Range 4,500 miles at 11 knots surfaced, 120 at 5 knots dived

Notes: Previously *Haddock* (K1), *Cachalot* (K2), *Orca* (K3), *Walrus* (K4).
K1, 2, 5 and 6 built by Fore River, K3, 7, 8 by Union Iron Works. K4 by Moran and Company.

K-5 (U.S. Navy)

U.S.A.

Type: Holland (7)
Class: "L1-L4", "L9-L11"
Dimensions, feet: 169 x 17.5 x 13.6
Torpedo armament: 4 x 18in torpedo tubes
Guns: 1 x 3in AA
Main machinery: 2 sets 650hp Nelseco diesels; 2 x 340hp electric motors
Speed, knots: 14 surfaced; 10.5 dived

Complement: 28
Dates: 1914-1915
Special features: Range, 4,500 miles surfaced; 150 at 5 knots dived

Notes: "L1-L4" and "L9-L11" built by Electric Boat Company. Cost £650,000.

L1 (U.S. Navy)

U.S.A.

Type: Lake (4)
Class: "L5-L8"
Dimensions, feet: 165 x 14.7 x 13.3
Torpedo armament: 4 torpedo tubes
Guns: 1 x 3in AA
Main machinery: 2 sets 600hp Busch Sulzer diesels; 2 x 400hp main motors
Speed, knots: 14 surfaced; 10.8 dived

Complement: 28
Dates: 1915-1917
Special features: Range 4,500 miles surfaced; 150 at 5 knots dived

Notes: L5 built by Lake T.B.Co. L6 and L7 Craig S.B.Co. Long Beach, California. L8 Portsmouth Navy Yard.

L6

U.S.A.

Type: Holland (1)
Class: "M1"
Dimensions, feet: 165 x 16 x 13.5
Torpedo armament: 4 torpedo tubes
Guns: 1 x 3in AA
Main machinery: 2 sets 8-cylinder 900hp Nelseco diesels

Speed, knots: 14 surfaced
Dates: 1915
Special features: Range 3,000 miles at 14 knots surfaced. 3 periscopes fitted

Notes: Built by Electric Boat Co.

M-1 (U.S. Navy)

U.S.A.

Type: Holland (3)
Class: "N1"
Displacement, tons: 348 surfaced; 414 dived
Dimensions, feet: 147 x 16 x 12.5
Torpedo armament: 4 torpedo tubes; 8 torpedoes
Main machinery: 2 sets 240hp Nelseco diesels; 2 x 280hp electric motors

Speed, knots: 13 surfaced; 11 dived
Complement: 25
Dates: 1916-1917
Special features: Range 1,500 miles surfaced, 120 at 5 knots dived

Notes: Built by Electric Boat Co. and Seattle Con & D.D.Co.

N1

U.S.A.

Type: Lake (4)
Class: "N4-7"
Displacement, tons: 350 surfaced; 420 dived
Dimensions, feet: 155 x 14.5 x 12
Torpedo armament: 4 torpedo tubes
Main machinery: 2 sets Sulzer Diesels
Speed, knots: 13 surfaced; 11 dived

Complement: 25
Dates: 1916-1918
Special features: Range 2,500 miles surfaced; 120 at 5 knots dived

Notes: Built by Lake T.B.Co.

U.S.A.

Type: Holland and Lake (10)
Class: "01-010"
Displacement, tons: 520 surfaced; 623 dived
Dimensions, feet: 172.5 x 18 x 14.4
Torpedo armament: 4 torpedo tubes; 8 torpedoes
Guns: 1 x 3in AA
Main machinery; 2 sets x 440hp Nelseco diesels; 2 x 370hp main motors
Speed, knots: 14 surfaced; 10.5 dived

Complement: 29
Dates: 1917-1918
Special features: Range 3,500 miles at 11 knots surfaced.

Notes: 01 built by Portsmouth Navy Yard, 02 by Bremerton Puget Sound NY; 03-010 by Electric Boat Co. and Fore River Co.
In addition 6 Lake type 011-016 were built by Lake T.B.Co. and Mare Island, NY.

O-1 (U.S. Navy)

U.S.A.

Type: Holland and Lake (27)
Class: "R1-R27"
Displacement, tons: R1-20 569/680; R21-27 495/598
Dimensions, feet: R1-20 186.2 x 18 x 4.5; R21-27 175 x 16.6 x 14
Torpedo armament: 4 torpedo tubes; 8 torpedoes
Guns: 1 x 3in
Main machinery: R1-20 2 sets 440 6hp Nelseco diesels; R21-27 2 sets 500hp Busch Sulzer diesels; R1-27 2 electric motors
Speed, knots: R1-20 135 surfaced, 10.5 dived; R21-27 14 surfaced, 11 dived
Complement: 29
Dates: 1917-1919
Special features: Range 4,000 miles at 10 knots surfaced

R-12 (U.S. Navy)

U.S.A.

Type: Holland Lake and Bureau Design (51)
Class: "S1-51" (ex S5)
Displacement, tons: 800-993 surfaced; 977-1,230 dived
Dimensions, feet: 207-240 x 19.5-21.7 x 16 13.5
Torpedo armament: 4 x 21in bow tubes (12 torpedoes) plus 1 x 21in stern tube with 2 torpedoes in S48-51
Guns: 1 x 4in (removed from some later)
Main machinery: 2 sets 600/100 diesels; 2 electric motors
Speed, knots: 15 surfaced; 10.5/12.25 dived
Diving depth: 200ft
Complement: 38

Dates: 1917-1924
Special features: Range 5,000 miles at 11 knots surfaced. 3 periscopes in S48-51

Notes: S1, 18-47 Holland type built by Fore River S.B.Co. Bethlehem S.B.Co. Quincy and Bethlehem S.B.Co. San Francisco. S3, 4, 6-13 Bureau Design, built by Portsmouth Navy Yard. S2 of smaller Lake type, S14-17 Lake type and S48-51 larger Lake type all built by Lake T.B.Co. Time from surface to periscope depth 60 seconds.

S45 (U.S. Navy)

U.S.A.

Type: Bureau Design (3)
Class: "Barracuda" (ex V1)
Displacement, tons: 2,025 surfaced
Dimensions, feet: 341.5 x 27.5 x 15.5
Torpedo armament: 4 x 21in bow; 2 x 21in stern; 16 torpedoes
Guns: 1 x 5in; 2 Lewis guns
Main machinery: 2 sets Busch Sulzer 2,250bhp main drive; 2 x 1,000bhp with generators for auxiliary drive and 2 main motors

Speed, knots: 21 surfaced; 10 dived
Dates: 1924-1925
Special features: Range 12,000 miles surface cruising

Notes: *Barracuda* (ex V1) *Bass* (ex V2) *Bonita* ex V3).
First US submarine designed for fleet operations. Designed to carry small sea-plane on after-casing when surfaced.

Barracuda

U.S.A.

Type: Minelayer (1)
Class: "Argonaut" (A1 ex V4)
Displacement, tons: 2,660 surfaced; 4,080 dived
Dimensions, feet: 381 x 33.5 x 15.2
Torpedo armament: 4 x 21in bow tubes
Mines: 6 in casing
Guns: 2 x 6in
Main machinery: 2 diesels of 3,175shp; 2 main motors

Speed: 14.6 surfaced; 8 dived
Complement: 86
Dates: 1928

Notes: *Argonaut* (A1 ex V4) built by Portsmouth Navy Yard, Machinery by Brooklyn Navy Yard. An improved version of the V1 class, being the first custom designed Minelayer for the USN. Total cost $6,150,000.

V4 (later Argonaut)

U.S.A.

Type: Patrol submarines (2)
Class: "Narwhal" (N1 ex V5)
Displacement, tons: 2,760 surfaced; 3,960 dived
Dimensions, feet: 371 x 33.3 x 16
Torpedo armament: 6 x 21in torpedo tubes
Guns: 2 x 6in
Main machinery: 2 diesels, of 5,447shp; 2 main motors
Speed, knots: 17 surfaced; 8.5 dived
Complement: 88

Dates: 1930
Special features: Carried 8 external torpedo stowage tubes in the casing

Notes: *Narwhal* (N1 ex V5) *Nautilus* (N4 ex V6). Built by Portsmouth and Mare Island Navy Yards with machinery from New York Navy Yard. Although authorised in 1916 as Nos 167, 168 these very large submarines were not laid down until 1927. Cost $6,370,000.

Narwhal (U.S. Navy)

U.S.A.

Type: Patrol Submarine (1)
Class: "Dolphin" (D1 ex V7)
Displacement, tons: 1,540 surfaced; 2,215 dived
Dimensions, feet: 319oa x 27.5 x 13
Torpedo armament: 6 x 21in torpedo tubes plus 3 torpedoes stowed externally
Guns: 1 x 4in

Main machinery: 2 MAN diesels of 4,300hp; 2 electric motors of 875hp
Speed, knots: 17 surfaced; 8 dived
Dates: 1932

Notes: Her size was more reasonable than that of her predecessor, being similar to that of the boats operating in World War II.

Dolphin (U S Navy)

U.S.A.

Type: Patrol Submarines (2)
Class: "Cachalot" (C1 ex V8)
Displacement, tons: 1,120 surfaced; 1,650 dived
Dimensions, feet: 271.8oa x 24.7 x 12.6
Torpedo armament: 6 x 21in torpedo tubes. No external torpedo stowage
Guns: 1 x 3in abaft conning tower
Main machinery: 2 sets Winton diesels of 3,100hp 2 main motors 800hp
Speed, knots: 17 surfaced; 9 dived

Complement: 45
Dates: 1934
Special features: Mainly welded construc...

Notes: *Cachalot* (C1 ex V8) *Cuttlefish* (C2 ex V9). First built by Portsmouth Navy Yard and the second by Electric Boat Company. Three smaller patrol submarines had their main machinery replaced under the 1936 programme as the original direct-drive main engines proved unsatisfactory.

Cuttlefish

U.S.A.

Type: Patrol Submarines (4 + 6)
Class: "Pike" and "Perch"
Displacement, tons: 1,310 surfaced, 1,934 dived
Dimensions, feet: 300 x 25 x 13
Torpedo armament: 6 x 21in tubes (4 bow, 2 stern, 16 torpedoes)
Guns: 1 x 3in abaft conning tower (see notes)
Main machinery: 2 Winton diesels of 4,300hp; 2 electric motors of 2,085hp
Speed, knots: 19 surfaced; 8 dived
Diving depth: 250 feet
Complement: 55
Dates: 1936

Special features: First all welded Submarines in USN

Notes: Portsmouth Navy Yard: *Pike, Porpoise, Plunger* and *Pollack*
Electric Boat Co: *Shark, Tarpon, Perch, Pickerel, Permit*
Mare Island Yard: *Pompano*
Two classes of slightly increased size to improve habitability for operations in the Pacific. All these boats ran on electric drive with two motors on each shaft in the "Pike" class, and four in some of the "Porpoise" class. A 4in gun was added forward of the conning tower in place of the 3in except in *Pike* and *Porpoise*, two 20mm were mounted on the bridge during the war and two external bow tubes were added in five of the boats.

Pike

U.S.A.

Type: Patrol Submarines (6)
Class: "Salmon"
Displacement, tons: 1,450 surfaced; 2,198 dived
Dimensions, feet: 308 x 26 x 14.3
Torpedo armament: 8 x 21in torpedo tubes (4 bow, 4 stern) 24 torpedoes carried
Guns: 1 x 4in (*Sturgeon* 3in); 4 machine guns
Main machinery: 4 diesels (2 per shaft); 4 electric motors (2 per shaft)
Speed, knots: 21 surfaced; 9 dived
Diving depth: 250ft

Complement: 70
Dates: 1938

Notes: Portsmouth Navy Yard: *Snapper, Stingray*
Mare Island Yard: *Sturgeon*
Electric Boat Co.: *Salmon, Seal, Skipjack*
This class reverted to composite drive with one diesel of each pair running a generator while the second was geared to the shaft. The twin electric motors drove each shaft through the same gear box. During the war the conning tower was cut down to mount two 20mm guns.

Salmon (U.S. Navy)

U.S.A.

Type: Patrol Submarines (10)
Class: "Sargo"
Displacement, tons: 1,450 surfaced; 2,350 dived
Dimensions, feet: 310.5oa x 27 x 13.7
Torpedo armament: 8 x 21in (4 bow, 4 stern); 24 torpedoes
Guns: 1 x 4in; 4 machine guns
Main machinery: 4 diesels of 5,500bhp; 4 main motors of 2,740bhp
Speed, knots: 20 surfaced; 8.7 dived
Diving depth: 250ft
Complement: 70

Dates: 1939-1940

Notes: Electric Boat Co.: *Sargo, Saury, Seadragon, Sealion, Spearfish*
Portsmouth Navy Yard: *Sculpin, Searaven, Seawolf, Squalus*
Mare Island Navy Yard: *Swordfish*
Machinery arrangements similar to "Salmon" class except in *Seadragon, Sealion* and *Seawolf*, which had geared diesel electric drive and single large main motor on each shaft. In May 1939 the *Squalus* sank on trials and was salved and re-named *Sailfish* in February 1940.

Saury

U.S.A.

Type: Patrol Submarines (6 + 6)
Class: "Tambor" and "Gar"
Displacement, tons: 1,475 surfaced; 2,370 dived
Dimensions, feet: 307.7 x 27.3 x 13.7
Torpedo armament: 10 x 21in tubes (6 bow, 4 stern); 24 torpedoes
Guns: 1 x 3in; 4 machine gunes
Main machinery: 4 diesels of 5,400bhp (2 per shaft); 2 GE electric motors of 2,740shp
Speed, knots: 20 surfaced; 8.7 dived
Diving depth: 250ft
Complement: 80-85
Dates: 1940-1941

Notes: Electric Boat Co.: *Tambor, Toutog, Thresher* ("Tambor" class). *Gar, Grampus, Greyback* "Gar" class)
Portsmouth Navy Yard: *Triton, Trout* ("Tambor" class). *Grayling, Grenadier* ("Gar" class)
Mare Island Navy Yard.: *Tuna* ("Tambor" class), *Gudgeon* ("Gar" class).
These two classes were of a new design being of double-hull construction with an external attack centre above the control room. Gun originally mounted abaft the conning tower but later moved to the fore-casing.

Thresher

U.S.A.

Type: Patrol Submarines (73)
Class: "Gato"
Displacement, tons: 1,526 surfaced; 2,424 dived
Dimensions, feet: 311.7 x 27.3 x 15.3
Torpedo armament: 10 x 21in (6 bow, 4 stern); 24 torpedoes
Guns: 1 x 3in; 4 machine guns
Main machinery: 4 Fairbanks Morse or GM or HOR diesels of 5,400bhp (2 per shaft); 2 main motors of 2,740shp
Speed, knots: 20.5 surfaced; 8.7 dived
Diving depth: 300ft
Complement: 80-85
Dates: 1942-1944
Special features: 2 engine rooms

Notes: Electric Boat Co.: *Gato, Greenling, Grouper, Growler, Grunion, Guardfish, Albacore, Amberjack, Barb, Blackfish,* *Bluefish, Bonefish, Cod, Cero, Corvina, Darter, Angler, Bashaw, Bluegill, Bream, Cavalla, Cobia, Croaker, Dace, Dorado, Flasher, Flier, Flounder, Gabilan, Gunnel, Gurnard, Haddo, Hake, Harder, Hoe, Jack, I apon, Mingo, Muskallonge, Paddle, Pargo.*
Portsmouth Navy Yard: *Drum, Flying Fish, Finback, Haddock, Halibut, Herring, Kingfish, Shad, Runner, Sawfish, Scamp, Scorpion, Snook, Steelhead.*
Mare Island Navy Yard: *Silversides, Trigger, Wahoo, Whale, Sunfish, Tunny, Tinosa, Tullibee.*
Manitowoc Sbdg.: *Peto, Pogy, Pompon, Puffer, Rasher, Raton, Ray, Redfin, Robalo, Rock.*
This class used diesel-electric drive with four generators supplying the two main motors, which drove through reduction gearing. The original 3in gun was mounted abaft the conning tower, but later moved forward in some cases being replaced by a 4in or 5in gun. Between the "Gar" and "Gato" class the *Mackerel* and *Marlin* of 1,179 tons were built as experimental boats.

Scorpion (U.S. Navy)

U.S.A.

Type: Patrol Submarines (127)
Class: "Balao"
Displacement, tons: 1,526 surfaced; 2,420 dived
Dimensions, feet: 311.7 x 27.3 x 15.3
Torpedo armament: 10 torpedo tubes (6 bow, 4 stern); 24 torpedoes
Guns: 1 x 5in (except some with 4in or 3in); 1 x 40mm, 1 x 20mm (in later boats); 2 machine guns
Main machinery: Fairbanks Morse or GM diesels of 5,400bhp (2 per shaft); 2 main motors of 2,240bhp
Speed, knots: 20.3 surfaced; 8.7 dived
Diving depth: 400ft except SS361-4 300ft
Complement: 80-85
Dates: 1943-1947

Notes: Portsmouth Navy Yard: *Atule, Balao, Bang, Billfish, Bowfin, Cabrilla, Capelin, Cisco, Crevalle, Pampanito, Parche, Picuda, Pilotfish, Pintado, Pipefish, Piper, Piranha, Plaice, Pomfret, Queenfish, Quillback, Razorback, Redfish, Ronquil, Sandlance, Scabbardfish, Seacat, Sea Devil, Sea Dog, Sea Fox, Sea Owl, Sea Poacher, Sea Robin, Segundo, Sennet, Spikefish, Sterlet, Tench, Thornback, Threadfin, Tigrante, Tigrone, Toro, Torsk, Trutta.*
Electric Boat Co.: *Apogan, Archerfish, Aspro, Barbero, Batfish, Baya, Becuna, Bergall, Besugo, Blackfin, Blenny, Blower, Blueback, Boarfish, Brill, Bugara, Bumper, Burrfish, Cabezon, Caiman, Capitaine, Carbonero, Carp, Catfish, Charr, Chivo, Chopper, Chub, Clamagore, Cobbler, Cochino, Corporal, Cubera, Cusk, Dentuda, Diodon, Dogfish, Entemedor, Greenfish, Halfbeak, Lagarto, Perch, Sealion, Shark.*
Cramp SB Co.: *Devilfish, Dragonet, Hackleback, Lancetfish, Ling, Lionfish, Manta, Moray, Roncador, Sabalo, Sablefish, Trumpetfish, Tusk.*
Manitowoc SB Co.: *Golet, Guavina, Guitarro, Hammerhead, Hardhead, Hawkbill, Icefish, Jallao, Kete, Kraken, Lamprey, Lizardfish, Loggerhead, Macabi, Mapiro, Menhaden, Mero.*
Mare Island Navy Yard: *Seahorse, Skate, Spadefish, Spot, Springer, Stickleback, Tang, Tilefish, Tiru, Trepang.*
Average time of construction, nine months. 10 lost during the war – 16 hulls cancelled. *Apogan, Pilotfish* and *Skate* used at Bikini 1946. *Sealion* and *Perch* subsequently fitted for troop landing, *Burrfish* for radar picket duties and *Guavina* as an oiler.

Balao (U.S. Navy)

U.S.A.

Type: Patrol Submarines (33)
Class: "Tench"
Displacement, tons: 1,570 surfaced; 2,428 dived
Dimensions, feet: 311.7 x 27.2 x 15.2
Torpedo armament: 10 x 21in (6 bow, 4 stern); 24 torpedoes
Guns: 1 x 5in; 1 x 40mm; 2 x 20mm; 2 machine guns (40 of the later boats had 2 x 20mm and no 40mm)
Main machinery: 4 Fairbanks Morse or GM diesels of 5,400bhp; 2 main motors of 2,740shp
Speed, knots: 20.3 surfaced; 8.7 dived
Diving depth: 600ft
Complement: 80-90
Dates: 1944-1946

Notes: Portsmouth Navy Yard: *Tench, Thornback, Tigrone, Tirante, Trutta, Toro, Torsk, Quillback, Argonaut, Runner, Conger, Cutlass, Diablo, Medregal, Requin, Irex, Sea Leopard, Odax, Sirago, Pomodon, Remora, Sarda, Spinax, Volador.*
Cramp S.B.Co. (Philadelphia): *Trumpetfish, Tusk.*
Electric Boat Co.: *Corsair, Unicorn, Walrus.*
Boston Navy Yard: *Amberjack, Pickerel, Grenadier, Grampus.*
The single 5in gun was mounted abaft the conning tower and in some boats a second 5in was added on the fore-casing.
A further 103 boats were either planned or ordered but cancelled in 1944 onwards. After the war the majority of these boats were converted under the Guppy (Greater Underwater Propulsive Power) programme giving higher dived speeds as a result of streamlining and greater battery power.

Quillback (U.S. Navy)

U.S.A.

Type: Patrol Submarines (6)
Class: "Tang"
Displacement, tons: 1,800 surfaced; 2,400 dived
Dimensions, feet: 269oa x 27 x 17
Torpedo armament: 8 x 21in tubes
Main machinery: Diesel electric with 16-cylinder radial diesels of much lighter weight per hp than previously
Speed, knots: 20 surfaced; 17+ dived
Diving depth: approx. 600ft
Complement: 78-83
Dates: 1951-1952

Notes: Portsmouth Navy Yard: *Tang, Wahoo, Gudgeon*.
Electric Boat Co.: *Trigger, Trout, Harder*.

The first post-war design with a much shorter hull contributing to increased dived speed. Some variations in fin lay-out.
Originally seven improved "Tang" class were scheduled but these were cut back with the onset of the nuclear building programme. *Grayback* was redesigned to fire Regulus cruise missiles and was completed as such in 1958. In 1967 she was converted as a troop transport capable of carrying 67 troops and their equipment. *Growler* started life as a Regulus Submarine and was due for conversion as a troop transport but this was cancelled in 1968. *Darter* was designed on similar lines to the "Tang" class and was the last of the more conventional diesel submarines.

Tang (U.S. Navy)

U.S.A.

Type: Patrol Submarine (1)
Class: "Albacore"
Displacement, tons: 1,500 surfaced; 1,850 dived
Dimensions, feet: 210.5 x 27.5 x 18.5
Main machinery: 2 radial diesels by General Motors and 1 Westinghouse main motor; single shaft
Speed, knots: 25 surfaced; 33 dived
Complement: 52
Dates 1953
Special features: see notes

Notes: *Albacore* was built by Portsmouth Naval Shipyard and had a hull of radically new design which has been followed in many subsequent classes. This is known in some cases by this boat's name. Used for many tests and trials which included the positioning of the propeller abaft the after control surfaces. In 1961 she started trials with a new stern configuration with dive-brakes amidships and a dorsal rudder. Further modifications up to 1965 included the installation of a silver-zinc battery and contra-rotating propellors.

Albacore (U.S. Navy)

U.S.A.

Type: Patrol Submarines (3)
Class: "Barbel"
Displacement, tons: 2,145 surfaced; 2,895 dived
Dimensions, feet: 219.5 x 29 x 28
Torpedo armament: 6 x 21in tubes
Main machinery: 3 Fairbanks Morse diesels of 4,800hp; 2 GE main motors; 1 shaft
Speed, knots: 15 surfaced; 25 dived
Complement: 79
Dates: 1959
Special features: see notes

Notes: *Barbel* built by Portsmouth Navy Yard, *Blueback* by Ingalls S.B.Corp., *Bonefish* by New York S.B.Corp. These were the last non-nuclear combatant submarines built for the USN and were designed on similar lines to *Albacore*. Originally the bow planes were mounted forward but subsequently they were transferred to the fin. All control arrangements were centralised in the attack centre, a plan adopted in all future submarines. Two radar picket submarines, *Sailfish* and *Salmon*, of 3,168 tons dived, were completed by Portsmouth Naval Yard in 1956 and the experimental submarine, *Dolphin*, of 930 tons and designed for deep-diving trials was completed by the same yard in 1968.

Bonefish (U.S. Navy)

Nautilus (Wright & Logan)
Sea Wolf (Wright & Logan)

U.S.A.

Type: Fleet Submarine (1)
Class: "Nautilus"
Displacement, tons: 3,530 surfaced; 4,040 dived
Dimensions, feet: 323.7 x 27.6 x 22
Torpedo armament: 6 x 21in tubes
Main machinery: 1 pressurised, water-cooled S2W nuclear reactor and 2 steam turbines of 15,000shp; 2 shafts
Speed, knots: 20 surfaced; 22 dived
Complement: 105
Dates: 1954

Notes: The world's first nuclear propelled ship *Nautilus* has a Guppy type hull and on 17 January 1955 originated the historic signal "Under way on nuclear power". She was built by General Dynamics (Electric Boat Co.). In her early journeys she averaged more than 20 knots dived and in July/August 1958 made the first Polar transit from the Pacific to the Atlantic passing under the North Pole on 3 August 1958. Her first refuelling took place in 1957 and her third core was replaced after 150,000 miles.

Almost simultaneously with *Nautilus* building, *Sea Wolf* was constructed with a different reactor design (Westinghouse S2G). Whereas the *Nautilus* reactor was a pressurised water plant that in *Sea Wolf* was a liquid sodium reactor. In December 1958 the sodium reactor which had given a great deal of trouble was removed and *Sea Wolf* was fitted with an S2Wa similar to that in *Nautilus*, recommissioning 30 September 1960.

U.S.A.

Type: Fleet Submarines (4)
Class: "Skate"
Displacement, tons: 2,570 surfaced; 2,861 dived
Dimensions, feet: 267.7 x 25 x 21
Torpedo armament: 6 x 21in tubes (4 bow, 2 stern)
Main machinery: 1 S3W or S4W nuclear reactor with 2 steam turbines 6,600shp; 2 shafts
Speed, knots: 20 surfaced; 25 dived
Complement: 95
Dates: 1957-1959

Notes: General Dynamics (Electric Boat Co.): *Skate*
Portsmouth Naval Yard: *Swordfish, Seadragon.*
Mare Island Yard: *Sargo.*
This class, the first production model nuclear powered submarines, were of similar design to *Nautilus* but smaller. *Skate* possesses two records. She was the first submarine to cross the Atlantic completely submerged, being dived for 31 days in all. On 17 March 1959 she was the first submarine to surface at the North Pole. These submarines conducted Polar transits and exercises during the period 1959-1969.

Sargo (U.S. Navy)

U.S.A.

Type: Fleet Submarines (6)
Class: "Skipjack"
Displacement, tons: 3,075 surfaced; 3,500 dived
Dimensions, feet: 251.7 x 31.5 x 28
Torpedo armament: 6 x 21in bow tubes
Main machinery: 1 S5W nuclear reactor with 2 steam turbines of approx 15,000shp; 1 shaft
Speed, knots: 20 surfaced; 30 dived
Complement: 93
Dates: 1959-1961

Notes: General Dynamics (Electric Boat Co.): *Skipjack, Scorpion.*
Ingalls S.B.Corp.: *Sculpin, Snook.*
Mare Island Yard: *Scamp.*
Newport News S.B. and D.D.Co: *Shark.*
This class was the first with the *Albacore* hull design using a single shaft. (The fore planes are set on the forward end of the fin and due to the hull form no stern tubes are fitted.)
In May 1968 *Scorpion* was lost south-west of the Azores having previously set an endurance record of 70 days dived.

Scorpion (Wright & Logan)

U.S.A.

Type: Fleet Submarine (ex Radar Picket) (1)
Class: "Triton"
Displacement, tons: 5,940 surfaced; 7,780 dived
Dimensions, feet: 447.5 × 37 × 24
Torpedo armament: 6 × 21in
Main machinery: 2 S4G nuclear reactors with 2 steam turbines, approx 34,000shp; 2 shafts
Speed, knots: 27 surfaced; 20 dived
Complement: 172 (as Radar Picket)
Dates: 1959

Notes: *Triton* was built by General Dynamics Corp. (Electric Boat Co.) and in 1960 circumnavigated the world remaining dived for 83 days and 41,500 miles at an average speed of 18 knots (except for landing a sick man at the Falkland Islands). She is the only US submarine built with 2 reactors and her first refuelling after 110,000 miles was started in July 1962. In 1961 her role as a Radar Picket was dropped, she was classified as an SSN and in 1969 was decommissioned.

Halibut, built by Mare Island Yard and commissioned in 1960, was the first submarine designed to fire guided missiles and the only SSGN to be completed for the U.S. In July 1965 she was reclassified as an SSN when the Navy discarded the Regulus programme. The Regulus II missile hangar in the bow was subsequently removed and at the same time the four other missile submarines were transferred to other duties.

Triton (U.S. Navy)
Halibut (U.S. Navy)

U.S.A.

Type: Fleet Submarine (1)
Class: "Tullibee"
Displacement, tons: 2,317 surfaced; 2,640 dived
Dimensions, feet: 273 x 23.3 x 21
Torpedo armament: 4 x 21in tubes amidships
Main machinery: 1 small nuclear reactor by Combustion Engineering Co. with single steam turbine and turbo-electric drive; 2,500shp; 1 shaft
Speed, knots: 15 surfaced; 20 dived
Complement: 56

Dates: 1960

Notes: *Tullibee* was built by General Dynamics (Electric Boat Co.) being originally designed as a 1,000 ton submarine. However the requirements of her reactor and other fittings increased her size during design. She was the first boat fitted with BQQ-2 sonar and her four torpedo tubes are set two aside. She cannot fire *Subroc* from these tubes and although showing a welcome cut in size, is not of the same efficiency as other submarines.

Tullibee (U.S. Navy)

U.S.A.

Type: Fleet Submarines (14)
Class: "Permit" (ex "Thresher")
Displacement, tons: 3,750 surfaced; 4,300 dived (some 4,600 dived)
Dimensions, feet: 278oa (295 in four) x 31.7 x 25.2
Torpedo armament: 4 x 21in amidships
Main machinery: 1 S5W nuclear reactor with 2 steam turbines of approx 15,000shp; 1 shaft
Speed, knots: 20 surfaced; 30 dived
Complement: 107
Dates: 1962-1968
Special features: *Subroc*

Notes: Portsmouth Naval Shipyard: *Thresher, Jack, Tinosa.*

Mare Island Yard: *Permit, Plunger.*
Ingalls S.B.Corp.: *Barb, Dace, Gato, Haddock.*
New York S.B.Corp.: *Pollack, Haddo, Guardfish.*
General Dynamics (Electric Boat Co.): *Flasher, Greenling.*
This class had a greater diving depth than previous boats and was the first to combine *Subroc* with the BQQ-2 sonar system.
On 10 April 1963 *Thresher* was lost off the New England Coast. Later submarines were delayed until enquiries were completed and new safety modifications and increased quality control of building instituted. *Jack* was fitted with twin contra-rotating propellors without reduction gearing. The hull was lengthened by 10ft to provide a larger turbine for this arrangement. *Flasher, Greenling* and *Gato* were fitted with heavier machinery and a larger fin than the remainder of the class.

Permit (U.S. Navy)

U.S.A.

Type: Fleet Submarines (37)
Class: "Sturgeon"
Displacement, tons: 3,860 surfaced; 4,630 dived
Dimensions, feet: 292.2 x 31.7 x 26
Torpedo armament: 4 x 21in amidships
Main machinery: 1 S5W nuclear reactor with 2 steam turbines approx 15,000shp; 1 shaft
Speed, knots: 20 surfaced; 30 dived
Complement: 107
Dates: 1967-1975

Notes: General Dynamics (Electric Boat Co.): *Sturgeon, Pargo, Bergall, Seahorse, Flying Fish, Trepang, Bluefish, Billfish, Archerfish, Silversides, Batfish, Cavalla.*
General Dynamics Quincy: *Whale, Sunfish.*
Ingalls S.B.Corp.: *Tautog, Pogy, Aspro, Puffer, William H. Bates, Tunny, Parche.*

Portsmouth Naval Shipyard: *Grayling, Sand Lance.*
Newport News S.B. & D.D.Co.: *Queenfish, Ray, Lapon, Hammerhead, Sea Devil, Spadefish, Finback, L. Mendell Rivers, Richard B. Russell.*
San Francisco N.S.Y. (Mare Island): *Gurnard, Guitarro, Hawkbill, Pintado, Drum.*
These boats have been modified under the subsafe programme established after *Thresher*'s loss. They are slightly larger than the "Permit" class and, therefore, probably a little slower. The fore-planes are mounted a little lower on the fin than previously to provide greater control and can be placed vertically for surfacing through ice. As well as the BQQ-2 sonar system, they mount a BQS-8 (primarily for under ice work) and BQS-13. They have carried out trials of the Harpoon anti-ship missile. *Hawkbill* has been modified to carry the USN Deep Submergence Rescue Vehicle (DSRV), a 50ft craft which can transfer personnel through the fore hatch.

Aspro (U.S. Navy)

U.S.A.

Type: Fleet Submarine (1)
Class: "Narwhal"
Displacement, tons: 4,450 surfaced; 5,350 dived
Dimensions, feet: 314 x 38 x 26
Torpedo armament: 4 x 21in amidships
Main machinery: 1 S5G nuclear reactor with 2 steam turbines of approx 17,000shp; 1 shaft
Speed, knots: 20 surfaced; 30 dived
Complement: 107
Dates: 1969

Notes: *Narwhal,* built by General Dynamics (Electric Boat Co.) is generally similar in design to the "Sturgeon" class. The S5G reactor is a Natural Circulation plant which eliminates the need for primary coolant pumps, the noisest components in a pressurised-water propulsion system (S5W) after the turbines.
Further attempts at silencing have been built into the *Glennard P. Lipscomb* (General Dynamics). This boat, the Turbine-Electric Drive Submarine (TEDS), is an advance on the Tullibee project and is designed for evaluation rather than as the prototype of a class. Dived speed is expected to be about 25 knots.

Narwhal (U.S. Navy)

U.S.A.

Type: Fleet Submarines (26)
Class: "Los Angeles"
Displacement, tons: 6,900 dived
Dimensions, feet: 360 x 33 x 32
Torpedo armament: 4 x 21in tubes
Main machinery: 1 nuclear reactor with 2 geared turbines; 1 shaft
Speed, knots: 30+ dived
Complement: 127
Dates: 1975 onwards

Notes: Newport News S.B. & D.D.Co.: *Los Angeles, Baton Rouge, Memphis, Cincinnati, Birmingham.*
General Dynamics (Electric Boat Co.): *Philadelphia, Omaha, Groton, New York, Indianapolis, Bremerton.*
Three submarines scheduled under the FY 1975 programme. It is reported that these large submarines will use a modified surface ship reactor. If this is of the D2G type, as used in *Truxton*, their rating will be approximately 30,000shp.

Los Angeles

U.S.A.

Type: Fleet Ballistic Missile Submarines (5)
Class: "George Washington"
Displacement, tons: 5,900 surfaced; 6,700 dived
Dimensions, feet: 381.7 x 33 x 29
Missile armament: 16 tubes for Polaris A-3
Torpedo armament: 6 x 21in bow
Main machinery: 1 S5W nuclear reactor with 2 geared turbines 15,000shp; 1 shaft
Speed, knots: 20 surfaced; 30 dived
Complement: 112
Dates: 1959-1961

Notes: General Dynamics (Electric Boat Div.): *George Washington, Patrick Henry.*
Mare Island Naval Shipyard: *Theodore Rossevelt.*
Newport News S.B. & D.D.Co.: *Robert E. Lee.*
Portsmouth Naval Shipyard: *Abraham Lincoln*

This class, of which the first three submarines were provided for in the FY 1958 programme, were built to a modified *Skipjack* design with 130ft added to provide for the 16 missile tubes and their ancillary equipment. They were initially armed with Polaris A-1 missiles with compressed air ejectors. They are now fitted with gas-steam ejectors for the A-3 missiles. *George Washington* carried out the first underwater launch of a ballistic missile from a US submarine off Cape Kennedy on 20 July 1960 and sailed on her first patrol on 15 November 1960. They are fitted with three Mark 2 Ships Inertial Navigation Systems (SINS). Two crews, Blue and Gold are provided for SSBNs alternating between patrols.

George Washington (U.S. Navy)

U.S.A.

Type: Fleet Ballistic Missile Submarines (5)
Class: "Ethan Allen"
Displacement, tons: 6,900 surfaced; 7,900 dived
Dimensions, feet: 410.5 x 33 x 30
Missile armament: 16 tubes for Polaris A-2 (to be modified for A-3)
Torpedo armament: 4 x 21in torpedo tubes (bow)
Main machinery: 1 S5W nuclear reactor with 2 geared turbines of 15,000shp; 1 shaft
Speed, knots: 20 surfaced; 30 dived
Complement: 112

Dates: 1961-1963

Notes: General Dynamics (Electric Boat Div.): *Ethan Allen, Thomas A. Edison.*
Newport News S.B. & D.D.Co.: *Sam Houston, John Marshall, Thomas Jefferson.*
This class was specifically designed for the SSBN rôle, being larger and better laid out than their predecessors. They will not be converted for Poseidon missiles. These are deeper diving boats than the *George Washington* with pressure hulls of HY80 steel.

Ethan Allen (U.S. Navy)

U.S.A.

Type: Fleet Ballistic Missile Submarines (31)
Class: "Lafayette"
Displacement, tons: 7,320 surfaced; 8,250 dived
Dimensions, feet: 425 x 33 x 31.5
Missile armament: 16 tubes for A-3 (24 converted for Poseidon)
Torpedo armament: 4 x 21in bow
Main machinery: 1 S5W nuclear reactor with 2 geared turbines 15,000shp; 1 shaft
Speed, knots: 20 surfaced; 30 dived
Complement: 140
Dates: 1963-1967

Notes: General Dynamics (Electric Boat Div.): *Lafayette, Alexander Hamilton, Nathan Hale, Daniel Webster, Tecumseh, Ulyses S. Grant, Casimir Pulaski, Benjamin Franklin, George Bancroft, James K. Polk, Henry L. Stimson, Francis Scott Key, Will Rogers*.
Mare Island Navy Yard: *Andrew Jackson, Woodrow Wilson, Daniel Boone, Stonewall Jackson, Kamehameha, Mariano G. Vallejo*.
Portsmouth Navy Yard: *John Adams, Nathanael Greene*.
Newport News S.D. & B.B.Co.: *James Monroe, Henry Clay, James Madison, John C. Calhoun, Von Steuben, Sam Rayburn, Simon Bolivar, Lewis and Clark, George C. Marshall, George Washington Carver*.
The last 12 boats of this class are officially classified as a separate class with very slight differences from their predecessors. *Daniel Webster* has hull-mounted bow planes. *James Madison* was the first Poseidon conversion completing in June 1970.
The Trident Project provides for ten large submarines eventually armed with the Trident I missile (range approx. 4,000 miles) to be operational from the late 1970s.

Lafayette (U.S. Navy)

U.K.

Type: Coastal Submarines (5)
Class: "Holland"
Displacement, tons: 104 surfaced; 122 dived (No 1); 150 dived (Nos 2-5)
Dimensions, feet: 63.3 x 11.7 x 5.5
Torpedo armament: 1 x 14in bow tube
Main machinery: 1 x 4 cylinder petrol engine 160hp (No 1) 250hp (Nos 2-5); 1 main motor 74hp
Speed, knots: 8 surfaced; 5 dived
Complement: 7
Dates: 1901-1903

Special features: Surface range 500 miles at 7 knots

Notes: All built by Vickers, Son & Maxim at Barrow-in-Furness. These, the first British submarines, were built to the American design of Mr. J.P. Holland of New Jersey USA and were almost identical to that used by the USN. No periscope was supplied and Captain Roger Bacon produced his own design. There were many early teething troubles but sufficient success was achieved for the Royal Navy to proceed with its own design for the A1. All the "Hollands" were disposed of by 1913, the first having been launched in November 1902, commissioning in 1903.

Holland No. 4 (R. Perkins)

U.K.

Type: Coastal Submarines (14)
Class: "A"
Displacement, tons: A1-4 165/180; A5-14 180/207
Dimensions, feet: A1-4 100 x 11.5 x 11.5; A5-14 99 x 12.7 x 11.5
Torpedo armament: 2 x 18in bow tubes
Main machinery: 1 petrol engine (12 cylinder 500hp A1-4, 16 cylinder 550hp A5-14); 1 main motor 150hp; 1 shaft
Speed, knots: 11 surfaced; 7 dived
Complement: 11-14

Dates: 1903-1905
Special features: A13 had a heavy oil engine fitted in place of petrol. Surface range 310 miles at 10 knots

Notes: All built by Vickers of Barrow. These were the first British designed submarines, having higher conning towers than the Hollands and a short periscope which projected its image on a mirror in the control room. A1 was the first British submarine lost by collision, in 1904.

A1 (R. Perkins)

U.K.

Type: Coastal Submarines (11)
Class: "B"
Displacement: 280 surfaced; 313 dived
Dimensions, feet: 135 x 13.5 x 12
Torpedo armament: 2 x 18in bow tubes
Main machinery: 1 16 cylinder petrol engine of 600hp; 1 main motor of 180hp; 1 shaft
Speed, knots: 13 surfaced; 8 dived
Complement: 16

Dates: 1905-1906
Special features: 15 tons of petrol carried. Surface range 1,000 miles at 8.7 knots

Notes: B1-11 all built by Vickers Barrow. This was a great improvement on the "A" class design, a number being operational during World War 1. They were the first British submarines to be fitted with fore-hydroplanes.

B9 (R. Perkins)

U.K.

Type: Coastal Submarines (38)
Class: "C"
Displacement, tons: 290 surfaced; 320 dived
Dimensions, feet: 135 x 13.5 x 12
Torpedo armament: 2 x 18in bow tubes
Main machinery: 1 16 cylinder petrol engine 600hp; 1 main motor 200hp; 1 shaft
Speed, knots: 13 surfaced; 8 dived
Complement: 16
Dates: 1906-1908
Special features: Surface range 1,000 miles at 8.7 knots

Notes: C1-16 C21-32 and C35-38 built by Vickers Barrow. C17-20 C33-34 built by Chatham Dockyard. These boats were later fitted with a W/T system and had longer periscopes (2) than the "B" class. These were fully operational during WW1 and also operated in the Baltic in 1918, three of them being blown up at Helsingfors. Two boats of a separate class, CC1 and CC2, built at Seattle for Chile, were acquired in 1914 by the Royal Canadian Navy. These were larger boats with a dived displacement of 373 tons and fitted with 5 x 18in torpedo tubes.

C33 (R. Perkins)

U.K.

Type: Patrol Submarines (8)
Class: "D"
Displacement, tons: D1 550 surfaced; 595 dived. D2-8 604 surfaced; 620 dived
Dimensions, feet: 162 x 20.5 x 14
Torpedo armament: 3 x 18in tubes (2 bow, 1 stern)
Guns: D4 was first British submarine to mount a gun. Subsequently most boats carried 2 x 12 pdrs.
Main Machinery: Diesel engines of 1,200hp; Main motors 550hp; 2 shafts
Speed, knots: 16 surfaced; 9 dived
Complement: 25
Dates: D1 1908; D2-8 1910-1911
Special features: Surface range 2,500 miles at 10 knots

Notes: D1-6 built by Vickers Barrow D7-8 Chatham Dockyard. This class was the first to use diesel engines and with twin screws. The conning tower was much larger than previously, giving the "D" boats a different profile. This class was also the first to have saddle-tanks instead of internal ballast tanks. In 1910 D1, taking part in exercises off the west coast of Scotland, succeeded in torpedoing two of the Blue Fleet cruisers after remaining undetected for three days. This was also the first class to have a W/T system incorporated in their design. The wireless mast had to be lowered by hand before diving. In fact the "D" boats were a tremendous improvement in all respects on their predecessors, being the first submarines with a proper patrol capability and at the same time providing improved living accommodation.

D4 (R. Perkins)

U.K.

Type: Patrol Submarines (57)
Class: "E"
Displacement: 660 surfaced; 800 dived
Dimensions, feet: 181 x 22.5 x 12
Torpedo armament: 4 x 18in (2 bow, 2 beam) in E1 type; 5 x 18in (2 bow 2 beam 1 stern) in E7 and E21 types
Mines: 20 in some (see Notes)
Guns: 1 x 6 pdr or 4in
Main machinery: 2 diesel engines of 1,600hp; 2 main motors of 840hp; 2 shafts
Speed, knots: 16 surfaced; 10 dived
Complement: 30
Dates: 1913-1917
Special features: Surface range 3,000 miles at 10 knots

Notes: Chatham Dockyard: E1 and 2, E7 and 8, E12 and 13
Vickers: E3-6, AE1 and 2, E9-11, E14-24
Beardmore: E25 and 26, E47 and 48 (with Fairfield), E53 and 54
Yarrow: E27
Armstrong Whitworth: E29 and 30, E39 and 40 (with Palmers)
Scotts: E31, E51
White: E32
Thornycroft: E33 and 34
John Brown: E35 and 36, E50
Fairfield: E37 and 38
Cammell Laird: E41 and 42, E45 and 46
Swan Hunters: E43 and 44, E49
Denny: E52, E55 and 56
E1 and E2 were originally laid down as D9 and D10.
These boats continued the saddle-tank design of the "D" class which was the first British design with internal bulk-heads.
This class was sub-divided into three sections – E1 (E1-6 and the RAN submarines AE1 and 2) E7 (E7-20) and E21 (E21-56). Of the E21 type, E28 was cancelled, and E24, 34, 41, 45, 46 and 51 were built as mine-layers with the beam torpedo tubes replaced by mine tubes giving them a capacity of 20 mines. All this class was disposed of by 1923.

E9 (S. Cribb)

U.K.

Type: Patrol Submarines (4)
Class: "V"
Displacement, tons: 364 surfaced; 486 dived
Dimensions, feet: 147.5 x 16.3 x 15
Torpedo armament: 2 x 18in bow tubes
Guns: 1 x 2pdr
Main machinery: 2 diesel engines 900hp; 2 main motors 380hp; 2 shafts
Speed, knots: 14 surfaced; 9 dived

Complement: 18
Dates: 1915-1916
Special features: Surface range 3,000 miles at 9 knots

Notes: S11 built by Vickers (V1-4). From 1914-1916 S1-3 of 386 tons dived displacement were completed by Scott's and W1-4 of 508 tons dived displacement were completed by Armstrong Whitworth, all being transferred to Italy in July 1916.

U.K.

Type: Patrol Submarines (3)
Class: "F"
Displacement, tons: 353 surfaced; 525 dived
Dimensions, feet: 151.5 x 16 x 15
Torpedo armament: 3 x 18in (2 bow 1 stern)
Guns: 1 x 2pdr
Main machinery: 2 diesel engines 900hp; 2 main motors 400hp; 2 shafts
Speed, knots: 14.5 surfaced; 9 dived
Complement: 18-20
Dates: 1915-1917
Special features: Surface range 3,000 miles at 9 knots

Notes: F1 built by Chatham Dockyard; F2 built by Whites; F3 built by Thornycroft.
These were ordered before the war but F4-8 were cancelled.

F2 (I.W.M.)

U.K.

Type: Patrol Submarines (14)
Class: "G"
Displacement, tons: 700 surfaced; 975 dived
Dimensions, feet: 187 x 22.7 x 18
Torpedo armament: 4 x 18in (2 bow, 2 beam); 1 x 21in stern
Guns: 1 x 3in
Main machinery: 2 diesel engines of 1,600hp; 2 main motors 840hp; 2 shafts
Speed, knots: 14 5 surfaced; 10 dived
Complement: 31

Dates: 1915-1917
Special features: Surface range 2,400 miles at 12 knots

Notes: Chatham Dockyard: G1-5; Armstrong Whitworth: G6-7; Vickers: G8-13; Scott's: G14.
The first seven boats had been ordered pre-war and the remainder in November 1914. G15 building by Whites, was cancelled in April 1915. These were the first submarines in the RN to carry 21in torpedoes.

G13 (R. Perkins)

U.K.

Type: Patrol Submarines (37)
Class: "H"
Displacement, tons: H1-20 364 surfaced; 434 dived. H21-52 440 surfaced; 500 dived
Dimensions, feet: H1-20 150.3 x 15.7 x 14; H21-52 171 x 15.7 x 14
Torpedo armament: H1-20 4 x 18in bow; H21-52 4 x 21in bow
Guns: 1 x 12 pdr in some boats
Main machinery: 2 diesel engines of 480hp; 2 main motors of 320hp; 2 shafts
Speed, knots: 13 surfaced; 10 dived
Diving depth: 180ft
Complement: 22
Dates: 1915-1919
Special features: Surface range 1,600 miles at 10 knots

Notes: Vickers Montreal: H1-10

Fore River Yard U.S.A.: H11 and 12 (H13, H16-20 were transferred to Chile in payment for Chilean ships taken over in 1914, and H14 and 15 were transferred to the RCN as CH14 and CH15)
Vickers: H21-32
Cammell Laird: H33 and 34
Armstrong Whitworth: H41-44
Beardmore: H47-50
Pembroke Dockyard: H51 and 52.
H35-40 building by Cammell Laird's, H45 and 46 by Armstrong Whitworth and H53 and 54 at Devonport Dockyard were cancelled in November 1917. This class was split between H1-12 built in North America to "Holland" class design and H21 onwards built in the UK. The latter were excellent submarines being the first fully armed with 21in toprpedoes. The first war loss was H10 in 1918 and the last was H31 in 1941. H34 and H50 were the last of this class to be scrapped in 1945.

H23 (Wright & Logan)

U.K.

Type: Patrol Submarines (7)
Class: "J"
Displacement, tons: 1,210 surfaced; 1,820 dived
Dimensions, feet: 275.5 x 23 x 16
Torpedo armament: 6 x 18in (4 bow, 2 beam)
Guns: 1 (or 2) x 3in (or 4in) mounted on a raised casing
Main machinery: 3 diesel engines of 3,600hp; 3 main motors 1,400hp; 3 shafts
Speed, knots: 19.5 surfaced; 9.5 dived
Complement: 44
Dates: 1916-1917
Special features: Surface range 5,000 miles at 12½ knots

Notes: Portsmouth Dockyard: J1 and 2; Pembroke Dockyard: J3 and 4; Devonport Dockyard: J5-7.
This class was designed as a result of the theory that submarines should be capable of operating with the main fleet. At the time *Nautilus* (later N1) of 1,694 tons dived was building at Vickers and designed to make 17 knots. *Swordfish* (later S1) of 1,475 tons dived was building at Scott's. She was designed to make 18 knots using steam turbines. However, neither of these boats ever became operational and *Swordfish* was converted into a surface patrol boat. Nor was the *J-class* any more successful in fleet operations and all were employed on patrol, the whole class, except J6 which had been sunk, being transferred to the RAN in 1919.

Nautilus (I.W.M.)

U.K.

Type: Patrol Submarines (18)
Class: "K"
Displacement, tons: 1,883 surfaced; 2,600 dived
Dimensions, feet: 338 x 26.5 x 16
Torpedo armament: 8 x 18in tubes (4 bow, 4 beam)
Guns: 2 x 4in; 1 x 3in in some; 1 Lewis Gun. (some mounted a depth charge thrower)
Main machinery: 2 Parsons or Brown-Curtis geared steam turbines; 10,000hp; 2 main motors 1,400hp; 2 shafts
Speed, knots: 24 surfaced; 9.5 dived
Complement: 55
Dates: 1916-1918
Special features: Surface range 3,000 miles at 14 knots

Notes: Portsmouth Dockyard: K1, 2 and 5; Vickers: K3,8,9,10 and 17; Fairfield: K4,13,14; Devonport Dockyard: K6 and 7; Armstrong Whitworth: K11 and 12; Scott's: K15; Beardmore: K16; Vickers/Chatham Dockyard: K26 (with 21 in torpedo tubes).

This class was the ultimate in the search for high-speed submarines to operate with the fleet. The fact that all had been disposed of within nine years (except K26) is a true comment on the total failure of this concept. Another indication of the gross misuse which this plan presented was the series of collisions by night off May Island in January 1918. Submarines are not capable of such operations and are too vulnerable for high-speed close-order surface operations. K26 was an enlarged version of her sisters and did in fact carry out a cruise to Colombo in 1924. K13, which foundered on trials in the Gareloch in 1917, was raised and re-numbered K22. K18-21 were re-numbered M1-4, and K23-25 and K27-28 were cancelled.

K12

U.K.

Type: Patrol Submarines (33)
Class: "L"
Displacement, tons: 870 surfaced; 1,055 dived. (L9 and L50 types 25 and 100 tons more)
Dimensions, feet: 231 x 23½ x 15 (L1). (L9 and L50 types 7 and 4 feet longer)
Torpedo armament: L1 Type: 6 x 18in, (4 bow, 2 beam); L9 Type: 4 x 21in bow, 2 x 18in beam; L50 Type: 6 x 21in bow
Guns: 1 x 3in or 4in (L1 and L9 Type); 2 x 4in (L50 Type)
Main machinery: 2 diesel engines of 2,400hp; 2 main motors of 1,600hp; 2 shafts
Speed, knots: 17.5 surfaced; 10.5 dived
Complement: 36 (40 in L50 Type)
Dates: 1917-1927
Special features: Surface range 2,800 miles at 10 knots

Notes: Vickers: K1-4, L11-22, L24-23 (with Chatham) L26 (with Devonport) L25 and 27 (with Sheerness)
Swan Hunter: L5, L33
Beardmore: L6
Cammell Laird: L7, L8
Denny: L9, L54 (with Devonport)
Pembroke.Dockyard: L10
Armstrong Whitworth: L52, L53 (with Chatham)
Fairfield: L55, L56
Whites: L69 (with Rosyth); Scott's: L71.
Of the L1 Type (L1-8) L1 and 2 were laid down as E57 and 58. Of the L9 Type (L9-12, 14-27, 32-33) L11,12,14,17 and 25 were built as minelayers, with 8 mines on each beam, in chutes. The 18in beam tubes were taken out of L14 and 17. L13 and 37-49 were not ordered, while L28-32, 34-36, 50-51, 57-68 and 72-74 were cancelled. There were many variations in profile in this class which was a popular successor to the "E" boats.

L27 (Wright & Logan)

U.K.

Type: Submarine Monitors (3)
Class: "M"
Displacement, tons: 1,600 surface; 1,950 dived
Dimensions, feet: 296 x 24.5 x 16
Torpedo armament: 4 x 18in bow (M1 and 2); 4 x 21in (M3)
Guns: 1 x 12in Mark X1; 1 x 3in
Main machinery: 2 diesels of 2,400hp; 2 main motors of 1,600hp
Speed, knots: 15.5 surface; 9.5 dived
Complement: 60-70
Dates: 1918-1920
Special features: See notes. Surface range 3,800 miles at 10 knots

Notes: Vickers: (M1 and 2); Armstrong Whitworth: (M3).
The building of K18-21 was halted in 1916-1917 when the Admiralty Committee on Submarine Development decided on the construction of Submarine Monitors. The fact that this crass idea got further than the conference table is another reflection of the failure to recognise the proper nature of submarine operations. With a 12in gun mounted forward of the conning tower the submarine had to surface to load. The muzzle was then shut off, the boat dived and, as a target passed, broached until the muzzle was clear of the water before firing. As it took only 25 seconds to broach, the claim was made that "the enemy" had no opportunity to take evasive action. What the target was to be is not apparent and whether it was possible to hit with one shot was never proved as none was ever fired in action. The 12in gun was removed from M2, which was converted into a submersible seaplane carrier but sank when she flooded through the hanger. M3 became an experimental minelayer carrying 100 standard mines.

M2 (Wright & Logan)

U.K.

Type: A/S Submarines (10)
Class: "R"
Displacement, tons: 410 surface; 500 dived
Dimensions, feet: 163 x 15.8 x 11.5
Torpedo armament: 6 x 18in (bow)
Main machinery: One diesel of 240hp; One main motor of 1,200hp; 1 shaft
Speed, knots: 9.5 surface; 15 dived
Complement: 22
Dates: 1918-1919
Special features: Surface range 2,000 miles at 8 knots

Notes: Chatham Dockyard: (R1-4); Vickers: (R7-8); Armstrong Whitworth: (R9-10); Cammell Laird: (R11-12). Ordered in December 1917. R5-6 cancelled August 1919.
This class was designed for anti-submarine operations for which role the hull-form was streamlined by fitting internal ballast tanks, removing the customary gun and the use of a single screw. 18in torpedo tubes were used to allow a bow salvo of 6. They arrived on the scene too late to prove their efficiency – **only one unsuccessful attack was carried out.**

R10 (R. Perkins)

U.K.

Type: Cruiser Submarine (1)
Class: "X 1"
Displacement, tons: 3,050 surface; 3,585 dived
Dimensions, feet: 350 x 29.7 x 17
Torpedo armament: 6 x 21in bow
Guns: 4 x 5.2in (Two turrets)
Main machinery: 2 diesels of 6,000hp; 2 main motors of 2,600hp; 2 shafts
Speed, knots: 19.5 surface; 9 dived
Complement: 110
Dates: 1924 (Commissioned 25 September 1925)
Special features: See notes. Surface range 12,400 miles at 12 knots

Notes: Built by Chatham Dockyard under 1921-1922 Navy Estimates.
Another "monster" resulting from the 1915 Admiralty Committee, conceived and designed before the full gamut of aerial and surface A/S measures had been developed. There was strong opposition to the concept and this, combined with endless problems with her main engines, caused her to be laid up within five years of commissioning. The havy gun armament was never repeated, nor was the double hull design except in the later minelayers.

X1 (Wright & Logan)

U.K.

Type: Patrol Submarines (9)
Class: "O"
Displacement, tons: 1,475 surface; 1,892 dived. (*Oberon* 1311/1805)
Dimensions, feet: 283 x 28 x 13.5
Torpedo armament: 8 x 21in (6 bow, 2 stern)
Guns: 1 x 4in
Main machinery: 2 diesels 4,400hp; 2 main motors 1,320hp; 2 shafts
Speed, knots: *Oberon* 13.5 surface; 9.5 dived. Remainder 17.5 surface; 9 dived
Complement: 56
Dates: *Oberon* 1927. Remainder 1927-1929
Special features: Surface range 8,500 miles at 10 knots

Notes: Chatham Dockyard: *Oberon, Odin*
Beardmore: *Olympus, Orpheus*
Vickers Armstrong: *Osiris, Oswald, Otus, Oxley, Otway*
This was the first fully post-war design and *Oberon*, the first of class, had many teething troubles. There were many new features in these boats – a greater surface range, 40ft periscopes, the use of the upper sections of the ballast tanks for oil fuel which, with the lower half for diving, gave quick diving times, the incorporation of an Asdic, twin stern tubes and strengthened pressure hulls. Unfortunately the light plating of the ballast tanks led to aggravating fuel leaks. This class was really made up of three types – *Oberon, Oxley* and *Otway* which started life in the RAN but were transferred to the RN in 1931 – the remaining six as improved "O" class.

Odin (Wright & Logan)

U.K.

Type: Patrol Submarines (6)
Class: "P"
Displacement, tons: 1,760 surfaced; 2,040 dived
Dimensions, feet: 289 x 28 x 13.5
Torpedo armament: 8 x 21in (6 bow, 2 stern)
Gun: 1 x 4in
Main machinery: 2 diesels of 4,400hp; 2 main motors 1,350hp; 2 shafts
Speed, knots: 18 surfaced; 9 dived
Complement: 56

Dates: 1929-1930
Special features: Surface range 8,400 at 10 knots

Notes: Chatham Dockyard: *Parthian*; Cammell Laird: *Phoenix*; Vickers Armstrong: *Pandora, Perseus, Proteus, Poseidon*.
Generally similar to the "O" class with certain improvements including a higher surface speed. *Perseus* was temporarily fitted with an experimental 4.9in gun which was later removed. *Poseidon* was lost in collision with a merchant ship off China on June 9th 1931.

Parthian (Wright & Logan)

U.K.

Type: Patrol Submarines (4)
Class: "R"
Displacement, tons: 1,740 surfaced; 2,015 dived
Dimensions, feet: 287 x 28 x 13.8
Torpedo armament: 8 x 21in tubes (6 bow, 2 stern)
Gun: 1 x 4in
Main machinery: 2 diesels of 4,400hp; 2 main motors 1,320hp; 2 shafts
Speed, knots: 17.5 surfaced; 9 dived
Complement: 51

Dates: 1930-1932

Notes: Chatham Dockyard: *Rainbow*; Vickers Armstrong: *Regent, Regulus, Rover. Royalist* (Beardmore) and *Rupert* (Cammell Laird) were cancelled in July 1929. In these classes certain upper deck features were incorporated to make conditions more pleasant on long service passages in the Far East – an upper deck galley and shower in the C.T. Although a wardroom bath was provided no corresponding increase in fresh water capacity was made.

Regulus (Wright & Logan)

U.K.

Type: Patrol Submarines (3)
Class: "Thames"
Displacement, tons: 2,165 surfaced; 2,680 dived
Dimensions, feet: 345 x 28 x 13.5
Torpedo armament: 6 x 21in bow
Gun: 1 x 4in
Main machinery: 2 diesels of 10,000hp; 2 main motors 2,500hp; 2 shafts
Speed, knots: 22.5 surfaced; 10 dived
Complement: 61
Dates: 1932-1935
Special features: Surface range 13,000 at 8 knots

Notes: Vickers Armstrong: *Thames, Severn, Clyde*.
This class was a return to the concept of the fast fleet submarines but because of increased fleet speeds only three were built. They were very large and comfortable, although costing over half a million pounds each.

Thames (Wright & Logan)

Sturgeon — 1st group (Wright & Logan)

U.K.

Type: Patrol Submarines (4 + 8 + 50)
Class: "S"
Displacement, tons: 3 groups 735/765/814 surfaced; 935/960/990 dived
Dimensions, feet: 202.5/208.7/217 x 24 x 12/12/13.3
Torpedo armament: 6/6/7 x 21in tubes (all bow except 1 stern in third group)
Mines: in lieu of torpedoes
Guns: 1 x 3in (except 1 x 4in in later boats of third group). Some had a 20mm gun on a bandstand
Main machinery: 2-8 cylinder diesel engines of 1,550hp; 2 main motors of 1,300hp; 2 shafts
Speed, knots: 14 surfaced; 10 dived
Diving depth: 200ft (250 in later boats)
Complement: 36
Dates: 1932-1945
Special features: Range 3,700 at 10 knots surfaced

Notes: Chatham Dockyard: *Swordfish**, *Sturgeon,** *Seahorse,** *Starfish,** *Shark,*** *Snapper,*** *Sunfish,*** *Sterlet,*** *Splendid,* *Sportsman, Shalimar.*
Cammell Laird: *Sealion,*** *Salmon,*** *Spearfish,*** *Safari, Sahib, Saracen, Seadog, Sibyl, Sea Nymph, Sickle, Simoon, Stoic, Stonehenge, Storm, Stratagem, Stubborn, Surf, Syrtis, Spirit, Statesman, Sturdy, Stygian, Subtle, Supreme, Seascout, Selene, Saga, Scorcher, Sidon, Sleuth, Solent, Spearhead, Springer, Spur, Sanguine. (Sea Robin, Sprightly, Surface* and *Surge* cancelled 1945)
Scott's: *Seawolf,*** *Satyr, Sceptre, Sea Rover, Sirdar, Spiteful, Strongbow, Spark, Scythian, Scotsman, Sea Devil, Seneschal, Sentinel.*
This was the first result of a decision to standardise on two main classes the medium sized "SS" class for North Sea operations and the larger and longer-legged "T" class.
The first group of four boats(*) was completed in 1933, and the second group of 8(**) in 1938. The first of the third group, P211, was launched in 1941. This was the first of the unnamed submarines, a practice which continued until Mr. Winston Churchill decreed that all submarines should receive names. P211 became *Safari* and all up to P229 were similarly treated. There was no P230 and P226, *Sirdar,* was the first launched under her own name.

Saga — 3rd group (Wright & Logan)

U.K.

Type: Submarine Minelayers (6)
Class: "Porpoise"
Displacement, tons: 1,750 surfaced; 2,150 dived
Dimensions, feet: 293 x 25.5 x 15.7. (*Porpoise* 288 x 29.7 x 13.7)
Torpedo armament: 6 x 21in (bow)
Mines: 50
Guns: 1 x 4in; 2 MG
Main machinery: 2 diesels of 3,300hp; 2 main motors of 1,630hp; 2 shafts
Speed, knots: 16 surfaced; 8.7 dived
Complement: 59

Dates: 1933-1939
Special features: Range 7,400 miles at 10 knots surfaced

Notes: Vickers Armstrong: *Porpoise, Narwhal, Rorqual*
Chatham Dockyard: *Grampus, Seal*
Scott's: *Cachalot* (P411, 412, 413 cancelled September 1941).
As the result of experience gained with M3 this class was designed for laying the standard Mark XV1 mine from a chain conveyor in the casing. These were comfortable and successful submarines although *Rorqual* was the only one to survive the war. *Porpoise* was identifiable by a break in the forecasing 60ft from the bow.

Porpoise (Wright & Logan)

U.K.

Type: Patrol Submarines (Small) (15+38+35)
Class: "U" and "V".
Displacement, tons: 3 groups 630/648/660 surfaced; 730/735/740 dived
Dimensions, feet: 191/197/204.5 x 16 x 14.5
Torpedo armament: 4 x 21in tubes (bow) (Four of the first group also had 2 external bow tubes)
Guns: 1 x 12pdr in first group, 1 x 3in in remainder
Main machinery: Diesel electric with 2 diesel generators of 615bhp and 2 main motors of 825shp
Speed, knots: 11.7 surfaced; 9 dived
Diving depth: 200ft (first and second group) 300ft (V class)
Complement: 37
Dates: 1938-1944
Special features: Range 4,050 miles at 10 knots surfaced

Notes: Vickers Armstrong (Barrow): *Undine, Unity, Ursula, Unbeaten, Undaunted, Union, Unique, Upholder, Upright, Urchin*, (P81-87 cancelled) *Vandal, Upstart, Varne, Vox, Venturer, Viking, Urge, Usk, Utmost, Uproar*, P32, P33, *Ultimatum, Umbra*, P36, *Unbending*, P38, P39, P41, *Unbroken, Unison, United, Unrivalled, Unruffled*, P47, P48, *Unruly, Unseen*, P52, *Ultor, Unshaken, Veldt, Vampire, Vox (ii), Vigorous, Virtue, Visigoth, Upshot, Urtica, Vineyard, Variance, Vengeful, Vortex*. (*Veto, Virile, Visitant, Upas, Ulex, Utopia*, cancelled February 1944).
Vickers Armstrong (High Walker): *Unsparing, Usurper, Universal, Untamed, Untiring, Varangian, Uther, Unswerving, Vivid, Vivacious, Vulpine, Varne (ii), Virulent, Volatile, Vagabond, Votary*. (*Unbridled, Upward, Vantage, Vehement, Venom, Verve*, plus 8 unnamed cancelled February 1944.)

Originally planned as unarmed "clockwork mice" for A/S training However, it was decided to fit torpedo tubes in case of war. These small and very handy boats were of single-hull construction with all fuel and ballast tanks internal. As a result of the gun being an after thought no separate hatch was provided for the gun-crew and the bridge became extremely crowded prior to, and after, gun action. This class bore the brunt of the submarine war in the Mediterranean and 21 were lost on patrol.

Ursula (Wright & Logan)

U.K.

Type: Patrol Submarines (15+7+31)
Class: "T"
Displacement, tons: 1,325 surfaced; 1,580 dived
Dimensions, feet: 274 x 26.5 x 16.3
Torpedo armament: First group, 10 x 21in (6 bow, 2 bow external, 2 amidships external firing forward). Later boats 11 x 21in (as above but with 1 external stern tube and amidships tubes firing aft)
Guns: 1 x 4in, 1 x 20mm in later boats
Main machinery: (1st group Vickers, Sulzer, MAN or Admiralty. Remainder Admiralty or Vickers) 2 diesels of 2,500hp; 2 main motors of 1,450hp; 2 shafts
Speed, knots: 15 surfaced (with luck); 8.5 dived
Diving depth: 300 in rivetted boats, 350 in welded boats
Complement: 60
Dates: 1937-1945
Special features: Surface range 8,000 miles at 10 knots in early boats and 11,000 at 10 in later groups

Notes: Vickers Barrow: *Triton, Triumph, Thistle, Triad, Truant, Tetrarch, Trusty, Turbulent, P311, Trespasser, Taurus, Tactician, Truculent, Templar, Tally-Ho, Tantalus, Tantivy, Telemachus, Talent (i), Terrapin, Thorough, Tiptoe, Trump, Taciturn, Tapir, Tarn, (Tiggerhaai) Tasman Talent(iii)) Teredo. (Theban, Threat* plus four un-named cancelled 1945)

Cammell Laird: *Thetis (Thunderbolt), Trident, Taku, Talisman, Tempest, Thorn, Thrasher*
Scott's: *Tribune, Tarpon, Tuna, Traveller, Trooper, Tabard (Talent (ii)* cancelled 1945)
Chatham Dockyard: *Tigris, Torbay, Tradewind, Trenchant*
Devonport Dockyard: *Thule, Tudor, Totem, Truncheon*
Portsmouth Dockyard: *Tireless, Token, Turpin, Thermopylae (Thor, Tiara* cancelled 1946-1947).
Of these boats, 15 in the first group, 7 in the second and the remainder in the third.

This was a splendid class of submarine, proving far more reliable than the preceeding "O", "P" and "R" classes. The enclosed 4in gun allowed a less disturbed platform for surface action whilst the bow salvo of ten torpedo tubes was the most numerous in any submarine. Eventually a stern tube was fitted and the two amidships tubes were turned aft giving a much needed stern salvo. With the arrival of radar an air warning set was fitted and, later, a surface warning set with a periscopic mast was added. Snort masts were introduced shortly after the war, the first speed trials being run by *Tradewind* in 1948. In 1951 the first "T conversion", *Taciturn*, ran trials in her new guise, with streamlined fin, lengthened hull to accommodate an additional battery section, new electrical system and the gun removed. Eight boats underwent this transformation, whilst five received a much reduced "Streamline" conversion.

Triton — 1st group (Wright & Logan)
Trespasser — 3rd group (Wright & Logan)

U.K.

Type: Patrol Submarines (15)
Class: "A"
Displacement, tons: 1,385 surfaced; 1,620 dived
Dimensions, feet: 281·6 x 22.3 x 17
Torpedo armament: 8 x 21in (4 bow 4 stern, 2 stern being external). 2 bow externals originally fitted. 20 torpedoes carried
Mines: 26 in lieu of torpedoes
Guns: 1 x 4in 1 x 20mm. (both later removed although 4in was replaced in Far East boats during Indonesian confrontation 1964-1967
Main machinery: 2 diesels of 4,300hp; 2 main motors of 1,250hp; 2 shafts
Speed, knots: 18 surfaced; 8 dived
Diving depth: 600ft
Complement: 60
Dates: 1945-1948
Special features: Surface range 10,500 miles at 11 knots

Notes: Vickers Barrow: *Alcide, Alderney, Alliance, Ambush, Amphion, Anchorite, Andrew, Astute, Auriga, Aurochs*
Cammell Laird: *Aeneas, Affray, Alaric*
Scotts: *Artemis, Artful*
Chatham Dockyard: *Acheron*
(Following cancelled: *Abelard, Acasta, Ace, Achates, Adept, Admirable, Adversary, Agate, Aggressor, Agile, Aladdin, Alcestis, Andromache, Answer, Antaeus, Antagonist, Anzac, Aphrodite, Approach, Arcadian, Ardent, Argosy, Asgard, Asperity, Assurance, Astarte, Atlantis, Austere, Awake, Aztec*).

This class was designed primarily for service in the Pacific, hence the high surface speed. All were fitted with surface-and-air-search radar, sonars and snort. Difficulties with *Amphion* (first of class) caused a bow-buoyancy tank to be built in. Over the years all these boats, with the exception of *Aurochs*, were streamlined with a high fin similar to the "T" conversions. This was a successful class, although liable to heavy rolling and, with an increase in electronic gear, difficult to air-condition. *Affray* lost in English Channel 16.4.51.

Alderney (Wright & Logan)

U.K.

Type: Patrol Submarines (8+13)
Class: "Porpoise" and "Oberon"
Displacement, tons: 2,030 surfaced; 2,410 dived
Dimensions, feet: 295.2 x 26.5 x 18
Torpedo armament: 8 x 21in (6 bow, 2 stern) 30 torpedoes carried
Mines: can be carried in lieu of torpedoes
Main machinery: 2 ASR 1 diesels of 3,680bhp; 2 main motors of 6,000shp; 2 shafts
Speed, knots: 12 surfaced; 17 dived
Complement: 68 (71 in *Porpoise* class)
Dates: "Porpoise" in 1958-1961; "Oberon" 1961-1967

Notes: Chatham Dockyard: *Oberon, Ocelot, Onslaught*
Cammell Laird: *Odin, Onyx, Opossum, Oracle, Finwhale, Grampus, Sealion*
Vickers Barrow: *Olympus, Orpheus, Osiris, Narwhal, Porpoise, Rorqual*
Scott's: *Opportune, Otter, Otus, Cachalot, Walrus*
In addition "Oberon" class have been built for Australia (4+2), Brazil (3), Chile (2), Canada (3).
These submarines, probably the best diesel-engined boats ever built, are notable for their silent operation.

Cachalot (Wright & Logan)

U.K.

Type: Fleet Submarine (1)
Class: "Dreadnought"
Displacement, tons: 3,500 surfaced; 4,000 dived
Dimensions, feet: 265.8 x 32.2 x 26
Torpedo armament: 6 x 21in
Mines: can be carried in lieu of torpedoes
Main machinery: 1 S5W nuclear reactor with geared steam turbines; 1 shaft
Speed, knots: 20 surfaced; approx 30 dived
Complement: 88
Dates: 1963

Notes: The first British built nuclear submarine, *Dreadnought* was built by Vickers Barrow with an American nuclear reactor from Westinghouse in collaboration with Rolls-Royce. Originally *Dreadnought* was to have had a British designed reactor but in 1958 the US Government agreed to provide an S5W, thus speeding up her construction. From the forward reactor compartment bulkhead the design is wholly British, including her long-range sonar and torpedo arrangements. She was the first British submarine to surface at the North Pole in 1971.

Dreadnought (Wright & Logan)

U.K.

Type: Fleet Submarine (2+3+5)
Class: "Valiant", "Churchill" and "Swiftsure"
Displacement, tons: 3,500 surfaced; 4,500 dived
Dimensions, feet: 285 ("Swiftsure" 272) x 33.2 x 27
Torpedo armament: 6 x 21in ("Swiftsure" 5)
Mines: can be carried in lieu of torpedoes
Main machinery: 1 pressurised water-cooled nuclear reactor with geared steam turbines; 1 shaft
Speed, knots: 20 surfaced; 30 dived (approx)
Complement: 103 (97 in "Swiftsure")
Dates: 1966 onwards

Notes: Vickers Barrow: *Valiant*, *Warspite* ("Valiant" class); *Churchill*, *Courageous*, ("Churchill" class); *Swiftsure*, *Sovereign*, *Superb*, *Sceptre*, *Spartan*, *Severn*, *S113* ("Swiftsure" class) Cammell Laird: *Conqueror* ("Churchill" class).
The nuclear reactor for these submarines was produced by Rolls-Royce and associates. These classes are broadly of the same design as *Dreadnought*, but slightly larger. On 25th April 1967 *Valiant* completed the 12,000 miles homeward passage from Singapore in 28 days, a record dived journey by a British submarine.

Valiant (Wright & Logan)

U.K.

Type: Ballistic Missile Submarine (4)
Class: "Resolution"
Displacement, tons: 7,500 surfaced; 8,400 dived
Dimensions, feet: 425 x 33 x 30
Missile armament: 16 tubes for Polaris A-3
Torpedo armament: 6 x 21in (bow)
Main machinery: 1 pressurised, water-cooled reactor with geared steam turbines; 1 shaft
Speed, knots: 20 surfaced; 25 dived
Complement: 141 (2 crews)
Dates: 1967-1969

Notes: Vickers Barrow: *Repulse, Resolution*
Cammell Laird: *Renown, Revenge*.
As a result of the Nassau agreement of 1962, the UK started a programme of ballistic missile submarines to be armed with American Polaris missiles with British nuclear heads. The original plan was for five of these submarines, but the fifth was cancelled on 15th February 1965 leaving the Navy with an inadequate number in the event of emergencies. *Resolution* was the first to commission, putting to sea on 22nd June 1967. Each submarine is manned on a two crew basis in order to obtain maximum operational time on patrol which is normally for approximately two months.

Resolution (Wright & Logan)

Note: torpedo tube diameters listed as 18in and 20in in earlier classes. Technically these were 17.7in and 19.7in respectively.

GERMANY

Type: Coastal Submarines (1+1+2+4)
Class: "U1", "U2", "U3", "U5"
Displacement, tons: U1, 238/283; U2 341/430; U3-4 421/510; U5-8 506/636
Dimensions, feet: Varying from U1 139 x 12.3 x 10.5 to U5 188 x 18.3 x 11.3
Torpedo armament: U1 1 x 18in (bow). Remainder 4 x 18in (2 bow, 2 stern)
Guns: 1 x 37mm in U3 and U5 classes. (1 x 4pdr added in U6 and U8 in 1915)
Main machinery: 2 heavy oil engines of (U1) 400bhp, (U2 and U3) 600bhp, (U5) 900bhp; 2 main motors, (U1) 400bhp, (U2) 630bhp, (U3 and U5-8) 1,040bhp; 2 shafts
Speed: knots: Surfaced U1 – 10.8, U2 13.2; U3 11.8; U5-8 13.4; Dived 9-10 knots
Complement: 22 (29 in U5 class)

Dates: 1906-1911

Notes: Germaniawerft Kiel: U1, U5-8; Danzig DY: U2, U3,4
Although three "Karp" class were ordered in Germany by Russia in 1904, U1 completed in December 1906, was the first U boat built for the German navy. From the start double hulls and twin screws were incorporated. The Germans very sensibly abjured the petrol engine and used Körting heavy oil engines. These, although they emitted clouds of exhaust and sparks through an upper deck exhaust, were much safer than the contemporary engines in British submarines. By 1908 suitable diesels had been evolved, to be used from the U19 class onwards.
The incorporation of stern torpedo tubes in these early submarines gave the Commanding Officers an advantage not achieved in the RN until the "D" class of 1910.

U1 (Drüppel)

GERMANY

Type: Patrol Submarines (4+3+1+2)
Class: "U9", "U13", "U16", "U17"
Displacement, tons: U9 493/611; U13 516/644; U16 489/627; U17 564/691
Dimensions, feet: U9 188 (U13 190, U16 200, U17 204.5) x 19.7 x 11.5
Torpedo armament: 4 x 18in (2 bow, 2 stern)
Guns: 1 x 37mm in U9 and U17; 1 x 4pdr in U13 and U16
Main machinery: 2 heavy oil engines of (U9) 1,000bhp; (U13 and U16) 1,200bhp; (U17) 1,400bhp; 2 main motors of 1,150bhp; 2 shafts
Speed, knots: 14/15 surfaced; 8/10.7 dived
Complement: 29
Dates: 1910-1912

Notes: Danzig DY.: U9-15, U17 & 18; Germaniawerft Kiel: U16
These were the last classes with heavy oil engines. U9 sank the British cruisers *Hogue, Cressy* and *Aboukir* on 22nd September 1914 resulting in an appreciation by many hitherto unconvinced people of the capabilities of submarines.

U13 (Drüppel)

GERMANY

Type: Patrol Submarines (4+4+4+11+8+6)
Class: "U19", "U23", "U27", "U31", "U43", "U51"
Displacement, tons: U19 650/837; U23 669/864; U27 675/867; U31 685/878; U43 725/940; U51 712/902
Dimensions, feet: U19 210.5 (U23 & U27 & U31 212.5; U43 213.3; U51 214) x 20.5 x 11.7
Torpedo armament: 4 x 20in (2 bow, 2 stern)
Mines: U43 and U44 acted as minelayers from 1916
Guns: 1 x 3.4in in U19, U23, U31, U43 and 2 x 3.4in in U27 and U51. (Some boats also mounted 4.1in guns during the war)
Main machinery: 2 diesel engines of 1,700bhp (U19) – 2,400bhp (U51); 2 main motors of 1,200bhp; 2 shafts
Speed, knots: 15 surfaced (U19 & U43); 17 (remainder) 9-10 dived

Complement: 35
Dates: 1912-1916

Notes: Danzig DY: U19-22, U27-30, U43-50
Germaniawerft Kiel: U23-26, U31-41, U51-56 (U42 unallocated)
These were the first classes to be engined with diesels. With the aim of attacking merchant ships the calibre of the guns was increased to allow the saving of torpedoes by surface action. A number of these guns were designed to fold sideways thus disappearing into the casing.
From U19 onwards net-cutters were provided as well as jumping-wires.

"U 19-51"

GERMANY

Type: Patrol Submarines (3+3+3+5)
Class: "U57", "U60", "U63", "U66"
Displacement, tons: U57 786/954; U60 768/956; U63 810/927; U66 791/933
Dimensions, feet: U57 & U60 219.7 (U63 224.3; U66 228) x 20.6 x 12.5
Torpedo armament: 4 x 20in (2 bow, 2 stern). 5 x 18in 4 bow, 1 stern in U66
Guns: 1 (or 2) x 3.4in (or 4.1in)
Main machinery: 2 diesels of 1,800bhp (U57 & U60) 2,200bhp (U63) and 2,300 (U66) and 2 main motors 1,200bhp
Speed, knots: Surfaced 14.7 (U57 & U60); 16.5 (U63 & U66); dived 8.4 (U57 & U60); 9-10 (U63 & U66)
Complement: 39
Dates: 1915-1916

Notes: A.G. Weser, Bremen: U57-59, U60-62
Germaniawerft, Kiel: U63-65, U66-70
The U66 class, completed in 1915, was built for the Austro-Hungarian Navy as U8-U12 but taken over by the Germans.

GERMANY

Type: Submarine Minelayers (2+2+5)
Class: "U71" (UE-1), "U73" & "U75"
Displacement, tons: U71 755/830; U73 745/829; U75 755/832
Dimensions, feet: 186.3 x 19.3 x 15.7
Torpedo armament: 2 x 20in (external)
Mines: 32 in 2 tubes
Guns: 1 x 3.4in or 4.1in
Main machinery: 2 diesels of 8-900hp; 2 main motors of 8-900hp; 2 shafts
Speed, knots: 10.5 surfaced; 8 dived

Complement: 32-39
Dates: 1915-1916

Notes: AG Vulkan, Stettin: U71-72, U75-80
Danzig DY: U73-74
These were two classes of long-range submarine minelayers to complement the large class of smaller UC boats. It is rumoured that HMS *Hampshire* with Lord Kitchener aboard was lost on a mine laid by U75. The second group, the UE-II, comprised U117-126.

U71

GERMANY

Type: Patrol Submarines (6)
Class: "U81"
Displacement, tons: 808 surfaced; 946 dived
Dimensions, feet: 230 x 20.6 x 13
Torpedo armament: 4 x 20in (2 bow, 2 stern)
Guns: 1 x 4.1in (U81-83); 2 x 3.4in (U84-86)
Main machinery: 2 diesels of 2,400hp; 2 main motors of 1,200hp; 2 shafts
Speed, knots: 17 surfaced; 9 dived

Complement: 38
Dates: 1916

Notes: U81-86 built by Germaniawerft, Kiel. No reason can be found for the reduction of the bow salvo to two but, apart from the "U99' class and the "U151", (Merchant) class this was the end of a plan which must have been both disconcerting for the CO and inefficient in its results.

U81 (Drüppel)

GERMANY

Type: Patrol Submarines (6)
Class: "U87"
Displacement, tons: 757 surfaced; 998 dived
Dimensions, feet: 215.7 x 20.5 x 12.7
Torpedo armament: 6 x 20in (4 bow, 2 stern)
Guns: 1 x 4in (plus 1 x 3.4in in U87-89)
Main machinery: 2 diesels of 2,400hp; 2 main motors of 1,200hp; 2 shafts
Speed, knots: 15.6 surfaced; 8.6 dived
Complement: 38
Dates: 1917

Notes: U87-92 all built by Danzig DY.

GERMANY

Type: Patrol Submarines (6)
Class: "U93" and "U96"
Displacement, tons: 838 surfaced, 1,000 dived
Dimensions, feet: 235.5 x 20.6 x 12.7
Torpedo armament: 6 x 20in (4 bow, 2 stern)
Guns: 1 x 3.4in ("U93" class); 1 x 4.1in ("U96" class)
Main machinery: 2 diesels of 2,400hp, 2 main motors of 1,200hp; 2 shafts
Speed, knots: 16.8 surfaced; 8.6 dived
Complement: 38
Dates: 1917

Notes: U93-98 all built by Germaniawerft, Kiel.

U93

GERMANY

Type: Patrol Submarines (6)
Class: "U99"
Displacement, tons: 750 surfaced; 952 dived
Dimensions, feet: 221.7 x 20.7 x 11.7
Torpedo armament: 4 x 20in (2 bow, 2 stern)
Guns: 2 x 3.4in (U100 1 x 4.1in)
Main machinery: 2 diesels of 2,400hp; 2 main motors of 1,200hp; 2 shafts
Speed, knots: 16.5 surfaced; 8.5 dived
Complement: 39
Dates: 1917

Notes: U99-104, all built by A.G. Weser (Bremen). Except for "U151" (Merchant) class, the last of the U-boats with only two bow tubes. Otherwise a handy and popular class.

U99 (Drüppel)

GERMANY

Type: Patrol Submarines (6+4)
Class: "U105" and "U111"
Displacement, tons: 798 surfaced; 1,000 dived
Dimensions, feet: 235.5 x 20.7 x 12.7
Torpedo armament: 6 x 20in (4 bow, 2 stern)
Guns: 1 x 4.1in; 1 x 3.4in
Main machinery: 2 diesels of 2,400/2,300hp; 2 main motors of 1,200hp; 2 shafts
Speed, knots: 16.4 surfaced; 8.4 dived

Complement: 36
Dates: 1917-1918

Notes: U105-110 and U111-114 all built by Germaniawerft Kiel, although the hulls of U111-114 were built by Bremer-Vulkan (Vegesack)
U115-116 were cancelled whilst building by Schichau, Danzig. These were to have been boats of 1,250 tons dived displacement.

U105 as French submarine (Drüppel)

GERMANY

Type: Minelaying Submarines (5+5)
Class: "U117" and "U122" (UE-II)
Displacement, tons: 1,164 surface; 1,612 dived (U122 1,470)
Dimensions, feet: 267.5 x 24.5 x 13.7
Torpedo armament: 4 x 20in. (bow)
Mines: 2 tubes for 42 mines
Guns: 1 x 5.9in (2 guns in some)
Main machinery: 2 diesels of 2,400hp; 2 main motors of 1,200hp; 2 screws

Speed, knots: 14.7 surface; 7 dived
Complement: 40
Dates: 1918

Notes: U117-121 built by A.G. Vulkan, Hamburg and U122-126 by Blohm and Voss, Hamburg. This was the second group of long-range minelayers, designed for operations off the US Atlantic coast and the first to carry the very large 5.9in gun.

U117 (Drüppel)

GERMANY

Type: Patrol Submarines (2)
Class: "U135"
Displacement, tons: 1,175 surface; 1,534 dived
Dimensions, feet: 274 x 24.7 x 13.7
Torpedo armament: 6 x 20in (4 bow, 2 stern)
Guns: 1 x 5.9in
Main machinery: 2 diesels of 3,500hp; 2 main motors of 1,690hp; 2 shafts
Speed, knots: 17.5 surface; 8.1 dived
Complement: 46
Dates: 1918

Notes: U135 and U136 built by Danzig DY. U137-138 of same class and the same builders were broken up in 1919 before completion.

U135 (Drüppel)

GERMANY

Type: Patrol Submarines (3+1)
Class: "U139", "U142"
Displacement, tons: 1,930 surfaced; 2,483 dived
Dimensions, feet: 311 x 29.7 x 17.3
Torpedo armament: 6 x 20in (4 bow, 2 stern)
Guns: 2 x 5.9in
Main machinery: 2 diesels of 3,500hp and 1 auxiliary charging unit of 450hp; 2 main motors of 1,780hp; 2 shafts
Speed, knots: 16 surface; 8 dived
Complement: 62
Dates: 1918

Notes: U139-141 built by Germaniawerft, Kiel. These were very large boats with a formidable gun armament and long range. They were also the first to bear names (U139 *Schwiger* and U140 *Weddigen* (of U9 fame)). U139 was retained in commission by the French Navy to whom she surrendered in November 1918, until 1935 being renamed *Halbronn*.

The subsequent class, "U142", was composed of U142-150 of which only U142 herself was completed one day before the Armistice. In many ways this class was similar to the "U139" although of 300 tons more dived displacement.

U139 (Drüppel)

GERMANY

Type: Ex-Merchant Cruisers (7)
Class: "U151"
Displacement, tons: 1,512 surface; 1,875 dived
Dimensions, feet: 213.3 x 29.3 x 18.5
Torpedo armament: 2 x 20in (bow)
Guns: 2 x 5.9in or 4.1in
Main machinery: 2 diesel engines of 800hp; 2 main motors of 800hp; 2 shafts
Speed, knots: 12.4 surfaced; 5.2 dived
Complement: 56
Dates: 1916-1918

Notes: Built (U151-157) by Germaniawerft, Kiel with hulls built at Flensburg, Hamburg and Bremen. The original design was to provide cargo-carrying submarines to penetrate the British blockade – in fact *Deutschland* (later U155) made two such trips to the USA. *Oldenburg* (later U151) was converted for naval operations. *Bremen* was damaged on her first voyage and converted into a surface ship, whilst U152, 153, 154, 156 and 157 were completed for naval service, two being sunk. Despite the need for maximum numbers for "unrestricted warfare" these must have been brutal boats to take on patrol with their slow speed and minimal torpedo armament.

U151 (Drüppel)

GERMANY

Type: Patrol Submarines (8)
Class: "U160"
Displacement, tons: 821 surface; 1,002 dived
Dimensions, feet: 235.5 x 20.5 x 13.5
Torpedo armament: 6 x 20in (4 bow, 2 stern)
Guns: 1 or 2 x 4.1in
Main machinery: 2 diesels of 2,400hp; 2 main motors of 1,200hp; 2 shafts
Speed, knots: 16.2 surface; 8.2 dived
Complement: 38
Dates: 1918-1919
Notes: All (U160-167) built by Bremer-Vulkan (Vegesack), being the last class of U boats completed at the war's end. Two (U162 as *Pierre Marrast* and U166 as *Jean Roulier*) were transferred to the French Navy, remaining in commission until 1935. U168-172 were broken up before completion. These boats are interesting because they show a return to the smaller type of submarine with a more reasonable gun-armament. The twelve boats of the "U201" class (U201-212) were similar to the "U160", whilst the "U229" class (U229-246), the "U247" class (U247-262) and the "U263" class (U263-276) were slightly smaller. None of these was completed. The "U173" class (U173-176) and the "U177" class (U177-200) of 2,790 tons dived displacement showed a return to the big boat idea, mounting 2 x 5.9in guns, whilst the "U213" class (U213-218) and "U219" class (U219-228) were of an intermediate size – 1,900 tons dived displacement – mounting four bow and four stern tubes in the "U219" with a single 5.9in gun. Again none of these were completed.

GERMANY

Type: Coastal Submarines (17 + 30 + 88)
Class: "UB"
Displacement, tons: UBI 127/142; UBII 263/292; UBIII 520/650 (508/639)
Dimensions, feet: UBI 92.3 x 9.7 x 10; UBII 118.5 x 14.3 x 12; UBIII 182 x 19 x 12
Torpedo armament: 2 x 18in (bow) UBI; 2 x 20in (bow) UBII; 5 x 20in (4 bow, 1 stern) UBIII
Guns: 1 x 2in or 3.4in (UBII); 1 x 3.4in or 4.1in (UBIII)
Main machinery: UBI: 1 heavy oil engine of 60hp; 1 main motor 120hp; 1 shaft; UBII: 2 diesels of 284hp; 1 main motor of 280hp; 2 shafts; UBIII: 2 diesels of 1,100hp, 2 main motors of 788hp; 2 shafts
Speed, knots: UBI 6.5/5.5; UBII 9/5.7; UBIII 13.5/8
Complement: 14-23-34
Dates: 1915-1919
Notes: UBI Series: "UBI" Class (UB1-8) Germaniawerft, Kiel; "UB9" class (UB9-17) A.G. Weser. (10, 12, 16 and 17 converted for minelaying with 8 mines in 4 chutes length 105ft).
UBII Series: "UB18" Class (UB18-23) Blohm and Voss; "UB24" Class (UB24-29) A.G. Weser; "UB30" Class (UB30-41) Blohm and Voss. (121ft, 274/305 tons); "UB42" Class (UB42-47) A.G. Weser (as "UB30" class).
UBIII Series: "UB48" Class (UB48-132) 48-53 Blohm & Voss, 54-59 A.G. Weser, 60-65 A.G. Vulkan, 66-71 Germaniawerft, 72-74 A.G. Vulkan, 75-79 Blohm & Voss, 80-87 A.G. Weser, 88-102 A.G. Vulkan, 103-117 Blohm & Voss, 118-132 A.G. Weser; "UB133" Class (133-141) surrendered or scrapped before completion; "UB142" Class UB142, 143, 148, 149 A.G. Weser; UB144, 145, 146, 147, 150-153, 155, 170, 178; 196 surrendered or scrapped before completion.
A busy and useful series of boats much employed in the Mediterranean and patrolling as far as the Irish Sea. The UBI Series and "UCI" Class were the only single screw submarines Germany built.

GERMANY

Type: Coastal Minelaying Submarines (104)
Class: "UC"
Displacement, tons: UCI 168/183; UCII 400/434 to 480/511; UCIII 491/571
Dimensions, feet: UCI 111.5 x 10.3 x 10; UCII 162-173 x 17 x 12; UCIII 185.3 x 18.3 x 12.5
Torpedo armament: UCI nil; UCII 3 x 20in (2 bow external, 1 stern); UCIII 3 x 20in (2 beam external, 1 stern)
Mines: UCI: 12 in 6 vertical tubes; UCII: 18 in 6 vertical tubes; UCIII: 14 in 6 vertical tubes
Guns: UCI: 1 MG; UCII: 1 x 3.4in; UCIII: 1 x 4.1in
Main machinery: UCI: 1 heavy oil engine of 90hp; 1 main motor of 175hp; 1 shaft; UCII: 2 diesels of 500/600hp; 2 main motors of 460/620hp; 2 shafts (UCIII same, 600/770hp)

Complement: 15-28-32
Dates: 1915-1919

Notes: UCI Series: UC1-8 A.G. Vulkan; UC9-15 A.G. Weser.
UCII series: UC16-24 Blohm and Voss; UC25-33 A.G. Vulkan; UC34-39 Blohm and Voss; UC40-45 A.G. Vulkan; UC46-48 A.G. Weser; UC49-43 Germaniawerft; UC53-60 Danzig DY; UC61-64 A.G. Weser; UC65-73 Blohm & Voss; UC74-79 A.G. Vulkan.
UCIII series: UC90-114 Blohm & Voss. (UC106-114 surrendered incomplete, 115-118 scrapped before completion).
In addition to these minelaying submarines UA (building for Norway) was taken over by Germany August 1914. The "UDI" class of large boats and UF series of small submarines were both cancelled.

UC1

GERMANY

Type: Coastal Submarines (2+6+20+8+16)
Class: "IA", "IIA", "IIB", "IIC" and "IID"
Displacement, tons: IIA 254/303; IIB 279/329; IIC 291/341; IID 314/364; IA 862/938
Dimensions, tons: IIA 134.3 (IIB 140, IIC 144) x 13.6 x 12.5; IID 144 x 16 x 12.7; 238 x 20.3 x 14 (IA)
Torpedo armament: 3 x 21in bow (6 torpedoes); 6 x 21in (IA)
Mines: 8 in lieu of torpedoes
Guns: 1 x 20mm (4 when on patrol); 1 x 4in (IA)
Main machinery: 2 diesels of 700hp; 2 main motors of 360hp (410 in "IIC" and "IID"); 2 shafts; 1,800hp/1,000hp (IA)
Speed, knots: 13 surfaced ("IIC" 12); 7 dived; 18/8 (IA)
Complement: 25; 43 (IA)
Dates: 1935-1939
Special features: Surface range 1,050/1,300/1,900/3,500 at 12 knots; 10 hours at 4 knots dived

Notes: "IIA" series: U1-6 Deutsche Werke Kiel.
"IIB" series: U7-24. Deutsche Werke Kiel, and Germaniawerft Kiel, Flenderwerft, Lubeck.
"IID" series: U120-121, U137-152 Deutsche Werke Kiel.
These classes were based on the UBII series of the First World War and were used for coastal operations and training. Chiefly employed in the North and Black Seas. U120 and U121 both building for Yugoslavia. Fuel in saddle tanks gave additional range in "IID" series.
U25 and 26 classified as type IA were built by Deschimag, Bremen in 1936. With a surface range of 6,700 miles at 12 knots these were the fore-runners of the later patrol submarines.

U26 — Type 1A (Drüppel)

GERMANY

Type: Patrol Submarines VIIC (556)
Class: "VIIA", "VIIB", "VIIC"
Displacement, tons: "VIIA" 626/745; "VIIB" 753/857; "VIIC" 769/871
Dimensions, feet: "VIIA" 211.7 x 19.3 x 14.5; "VIIB" 218.3 x 20.3 x 15.5; "VIIC" 220.3 x 20.3 x 15.7
Torpedo armament: 5 tubes (4 bow, 1 stern) (11/12/14 torpedoes carried)
Mines: 14 could be carried in lieu of torpedoes
Guns: Originally 1 x 3.5in and 1 x 20mm, later increased in some boats by 1 x 37mm and up to 3 x 20mm, the 3.5in being removed for the latter addition
Main machinery: 2 diesels of 2,100hp (VIIIA) or 2,800hp (VIIB & C); 2 main motors of 750hp; 2 shafts
Speed, knots: 16-17 surfaced; 8 dived
Complement: 44
Dates: 1936-1943
Special features: Surface range (4,300 "VIIA") 6,500 at 12 knots; dived 20 hours at 4 knots

Notes: Type VIIA: U27-32 A.G. Weser; U33-36 Germaniawerft.
Type VIIB: U45-55, U99-102 Germaniawerft; U73-76 Blohm & Voss; U83-87 Flenderwerft
Type VIIC: U69-72, U93-98, U201-202, U221-232, U235-250 U1051-1058, U1063-1065, Germaniawerft; U77-82, U132-136, U251-300, U551-650, U951-1047, Blohm & Voss; U88-92, U301-330, U903-904, Flenderwerft; U331-349 Nord Seewerke; U350-370 Flensburg; U371-400, U651-683, Howaldtswerke; U401-430, U451-458, U465-486 Danzig DY.; U431-450, U731-750, U825-828, U835-836, Schichau (Danzig); U701-722, U905-908 Stülcken; U751-779 Wilhelmshaven DY.; U821-822 Stettin; U901 Vulkan Stettin; U921-930 Rostock.

These boats were probably the hardest worked of any class during the war and with those on the following page underwent many variations from their first building in 1936. They had external fuel tanks which were enlarged in VIIB and C whilst two extra reloads were carried externally in VIIC. One major disadvantage of this class was the external stowage of H.P. air bottles, liable to fracture and explode during depth charge attack. With twin rudders they were extremely handy on the surface.

U1202 — Type VIIc — as Norwegian *Kinn* (Wright & Logan)

GERMANY

Type: Patrol Submarines (72)
Class: "VIIC" (41-2) "VIID" & "VIIF"
Displacement, tons: "VIIC" (41-2) 769/871; "VIID" 965/1080; "VIIF" 1084/1181
Dimensions, feet: "VIIC" (41-2) 220.3 x 20.3 x 15.7; "VIID" 252.3 x 21 x 16.5; "VIIF" 254.7 x 24 x 16
Torpedo armament: 5 x 21in (4 bow, 1 stern) (14 torpedoes)
Mines: 14 in lieu of torpedoes ("VIIC" (41-2). "VIID" additional 15 mines or 39 in lieu of all torpedoes
Guns: 1 x 3.5in in "VIIC" (41.2). 1 to 4 x 37mm and 1 to 4 x 20mm in all boats
Main machinery: 2 diesels of 2,800bhp; 2 main motors of 750bhp; 2 shafts
Speed, knots: 16-17 surfaced; 7.5-8 dived
Complement: 44-46

Notes: VIIC (41-2): U1101-1110 Nord See Werke; U1131-1132 Howaldtswerke; U1161-1172 Danzig; U1191-1210 and U1217 Schichau; U1271-1279 Bremer Vulkan; U1301-1308 Flensburg.
VIID: U213-218 Germaniawerft.
VIIF: U1059 x 1062 Germaniawerftse.
Type "VIIC" (41-2) was basically the "VIIC" with a strengthened pressure hull.
Type "VIIC" (42), none of which was ever completed, was to have had further pressure hull strengthening, an armoured conning tower, increased A.A. armament and increased range. The "VIID" was lengthened by 32ft to give space for five free-flooding mine shafts on the centre-line each accommodating three mines. The range was increased with larger tanks but with some loss of speed.
"VIIF", approximately the same size as "VIID", had the additional midships section fitted with a hatch for the stowage of a cargo of 25 torpedoes to replenish other boats at sea.

VIIC type (Drüppel)

GERMANY

Type: Patrol Submarines (210)
Class: "IXA", "IXB", "IXC", "IXC40", "IXD (1 & 2)"
Displacement, tons: "IXA" 1032/1153; "IXB" 1051/1178; "IXC" 1120/1232; "IXC" (40) 1144/1247; "IXD" 1615/1800
Dimensions, feet: 251 x 22 x 15.5 ("IXD" 287.5 x 24.5 x 17.7)
Torpedo armament: 6 x 21in tubes (4 bow, 2 stern) except "IXD (1)". 22 torpedoes or, in most cases, 6 torpedoes and 32 mines
Guns: 1 x 4.1in; 1 x 37mm; 1 or 2 x 20mm ("IXD" (1)-1 x 37mm and 4 x 20mm only)
Main machinery: 2 diesels of 440bhp (In "IXA", "B" and "C"), 2,800bhp (in "IXD (1)") 5,400 (In "IXD (2)"); 2 main motors of 1,000shp, 1,100 in "IXD (1)" and "(2)"; 2 shafts
Speed, knots: 18.3 surfaced "IXA", "B" and "C", 15.7 in "IXD (1)", 19.3 in "IXD (2)" 7-7.3 dived
Complement: 48 "IXA", "B" and "C". 57 "IXD (1) and (2)"
Special features: Surface range "IXA" 8,100 miles at 12 knots, "IXB" 8,700 at 12 knots, "IXC" 11,000 at 12 knots, "IXD (1)" 9,900 at 12 knots, "IXD (2)" 23,700 at 12 knots. Dived 15-26 hours at 4 knots.

Notes: IXA: U37-44 A.G. Weser.
IXB: U64-65, U103-111, U112-124, A.G. Weser.
IXC: U66-U68, U125-131, U153-160, U171-176, U183-194, U841-846, U853-858, U865-870, U877-881, U889 A.G. Weser; U161-170, U801-806 Bremerhaven; U501-550, U1221-1238 Deutschewerft.
IXD: (1) U180 and 195 A.G. Weser.
IXD: (2) U177-179, U181 and 182, U196-200, U847-852, U859-864, U871-876, U883-886, A.G. Weser.
With their long range and greatly increased torpedo/mine load, these boats were particularly valuable on long range patrols. Extra fuel was carried in the later boats and in the two types IXD (1) the original six fast diesels were replaced by two slow-running diesels. In the type IXD (2) two slow-running diesels were coupled to each shaft and provision made for fitting eight vertical mineshafts (each with four mines) in place of reload. Some of these boats were used for importing vital stocks from Japan and U80 and U195 (submarine tankers) for importing fuel.
Transfers to Japanese Navy-U511 (RO500), U1224 (R501), U181 (I501), U862 (I502), U195 (I506)

GERMANY

Type: Minelaying and Cruiser Submarines (8)
Class: "XB" and "XI"
Displacement, tons: 1,763 surfaced; 2,177 dived
Dimensions, feet: 294.7 x 30.3 x 13.5
Torpedo armament: 2 x 21in (stern)
Mines: 66 (18 in 6 internal chutes forward and 48 in 24 external chutes, 12 on each beam)
Guns: 1 x 4.1in; 1 x 37mm; 1 x 20mm (later 4 x 20mm with 4.1in removed)
Main machinery: 2 diesels of 4,200bhp; 2 main motors of 1,100shp; 2 shafts
Speed, knots: 16.5 surfaced; 7 dived
Complement: 52
Dates: 1941-1943
Special features: Range 14,500 at 12 knots surfaced. 24 hours at 4 knots dived.

Notes: U116-119, U219 & 220, U233 & 234 Germaniawerft, Kiel. This design was an improvement on the XA which was never put into production. Reload torpedoes in both internal and external stowages. Despite their mine-laying capability these boats were frequently used as supply ships. U219 was transferred to Japan in 1945 as I505.

The next class in numerical sequence, the "XI" (U113-115), were designed as heavily-armed cruisers with a large range. They were to have mounted four 5in. guns with 8 torpedo tubes and an aircraft. Very wisely this design was dropped.

GERMANY

Type: Submarine Tankers (10)
Class: "XIV"
Displacement, tons: 1,688 surfaced; 1,932 dived
Dimensions, feet: 220.3 x 30.7 x 21.3
Torpedo armament: Nil
Guns: 2 x 37mm; 1 x 20mm
Main machinery: 2 diesels of 2,800bhp; 2 main motors of 750shp; 2 shafts
Speed, knots: 14.5 surfaced; 6.3 dived
Complement: 53
Dates: 1942-1943
Special features: Range 9,300 at 12 knots surfaced, 14 hours at 4 knots dived.

Notes: U459-464 and U487-490 Deutsche Werke, Kiel.
This was a shorter and more beamy class than the "IXD (1)" with a greater cargo capacity, being able to carry 430 tons of fuel as well as four torpedos externally. The entire class of 10 was sunk during the war.
Type "XV", a triple cylinder hull class of about 2,500 tons and the type "XVI" of about 5,000 tons were proposed for supply duties. In view of the fate of the type "XIV"s the decision to cancel these types was clearly correct.

GERMANY

Type: Coastal Submarines (4+3)
Class: "XVIIA" and "XVIIB"
Displacement, tons: "XVIIA" 236/259 dived; "XVIIB" 312 surfaced, 357 dived
Dimensions, feet: "XVIIA" 111.5 x 11.3 x 15; "XVIIB" 136.3 x 11.3 x 14
Torpedo armament: 2 x 21in tubes (bow and 4 torpedoes)
Main machinery: 1 diesel of 210bhp; 1 main motor of 77şhp; 1 Walther geared turbine of 5,000shp (2,500shp in "XVIIB"); 1 shaft
Speed, knots: 9 surfaced; 5 dived. 26 knots dived on turbines (21.5 knots in "XVIIB")
Complement: 12-19
Dates: 1943-1944
Special features: Range 1,840 miles at 9 knots surfaced; 9 hours at 4.5 knots dived. 3 hours at 26 knots (6 hours at 20 knots in "XVIIB") dived on turbines.

Notes: "XVIIA": U792 and U793 Blohm and Voss; U794 and 795 Germaniawerft.
"XVIIB": U1405-1407 Blohm and Voss (U1408-1416 cancelled).
The Walther turbine, which was a closed cycle engine running on High Test Peroxide, was first tried out at sea in the V80 of 80 tons. She was launched in 1940 and the U791 (ex V300) was to have followed in 1942. However she was never completed and the Walther turbines were built into the larger type XVIIs. These were all scuttled at the end of the war, some being salved later and one (U1407) was commissioned in the Royal Navy as HMS Meteorite running trials until she was scrapped in 1950. V80 was therefore the first true submarine. Further type XVIIs G with Walther turbines and K with a closed cycle diesel running on Ingolin were abandoned. Type XVIII with three shafts and Walther turbines was also discarded as the type XXI was developed.

GERMANY

Type: Patrol Submarines (124)
Class: "XXI"
Displacement, tons: 1,621 surfaced; 1,819 dived
Dimensions, feet: 251.7 x 21.7 x 20.3
Torpedo armament: 6 x 21in tubes (bow) 23 torpedoes or 12 torpedoes and 12 mines
Guns: 4 x 20mm (designed for 3 x 30mm). Faired in pairs forward and aft of the conning tower.
Main machinery: 2 diesels of 4,000bhp; 2 main motors of 5,000shp; 2 auxiliary drive motors of 226shp; 2 shafts
Speed, knots: 15.5 surfaced; 16 dived on main motors, 5 on auxiliary drive
Complement: 57
Dates: 1944-1945
Special features: Range 11,150 miles at 12 knots surfaced; 48 hours at 6 knots dived
Notes: U2501-2546, U2548 & 2551 Blohm and Voss (remainder of numbers to 3000 cancelled or scrapped) U3001-U3035, U3037-3044, U3047, U3050 & U3051 A.G. Weser, Bremen (Remainder of numbers to 3500 cancelled or scrapped). U3501-3530 Schichan, Danzig (remainder of numbers to 4000 scrapped or cancelled except for U3538-3542 plus an unknown number completed for USSR).

This was a revolution in submarine design giving the highest under-water speed yet known for a diesel submarine. The battery capacity was trebled compared with previous boats giving two days endurance at 6 knots and one hour at full speed dived. With very satisfactory streamlining and a periscopic snort-mast a speed of 12 knots snorting was available. If these magnificant submarines had come into production a year earlier they might well have caused very great losses in the North Atlantic. In fact very few actually got on patrol, the majority of completed boats being scuttled. Improvements on the type "XXI" were planned, "XXIB" having six extra torpedo tubes trained aft and "XXIC" increasing this number to an extra 12 tubes. Design studies were in hand for the "XXID", "XXIE", "XXIT" and "XXIV" all to be used as supply submarines. These projects were dropped.

U2518 — Type XXI — as the French Roland Morrilot (Wright & Logan)

GERMANY

Type: Coastal Submarines (56)
Class: "XXIII"
Displacement, tons: 232 surfaced; 256 dived
Dimensions, feet: 112 x 9.7 x 12.3
Torpedo armament: 2 x 21in tubes (bow)
Main machinery: 1 diesel of 580bhp; 1 main motor of 600 ship; 1 auxiliary drive of 35shp; 1 shaft
Speed, knots: 9.7 surfaced; 12.3 dived. 2 on auxiliary drive
Complement: 14
Dates: 1944-1945
Special features: Range 1,350 miles at 9.7 knots surfaced; 44 hours at 4 knots dived

Notes: U2321-2331, U2334-2371 Deutschewerft, Hamburg. U4701-4707 and U4710 Germaniawerft, Kiel. Remainder of numbers U2372-2500, U4001-4500 and U4711-5000 were scrapped or cancelled.

This class of diminutive submarines, of which very few got on patrol, was designed for inshore operations and plans had been laid for their building in many occupied shipyards. They had no casing over the pressure hull and the two torpedo tubes had to be loaded from forward with the boat trimmed by the stern.

Numerous other classes had been designed but none was continued in production. "XXII" of 200 tons with a Walther turbine; "XXIV" of 1,900 tons with 2 Walther turbines; "XXV", "XXVI" a smaller edition of "XXIV", "XXVIII" of 200 tons with steam turbines; "XXIXA"-"K" variations on a basic 700 ton hull with diesel electric or closed cycle diesel propulsion and up to 12 torpedo tubes; "XXX" and "XXXI" similar types of 1,200 ton boats; "XXXIII" of 360 tons; "XXXIV" of 1,400 tons; "XXXV" of 850 tons with Walther Turbines; "XXXVI" of 930 tons with four closed cycle diesels giving 22 knots.

U2326 (I.W.M.)

GERMANY

Type: Patrol Submarines (3+6+18)
Class: "201", "205", "206"
Displacement, tons: "201" and "205", 370 surfaced; 450 dived. "206", 500 surfaced; 600 dived
Dimensions, feet: 142.7 x 15.1 x 13.5 ("201" and "205"); 147.6 x 15.4 x 13.8 ("206")
Torpedo armament: 8 x 21in (bow)
Mines: Can lay mines
Main machinery: 2 diesels of 1,200bhp ("201" and "205") 1,800bhp ("206"); 2 main motors of 1,700bhp; 1 shaft
Speed, knots: 10 surfaced; 17 dived
Complement: 21
Dates: 1962-1974

Notes: U1-12 Howaldtswerke, Kiel; U13-30 Howaldtswerke and Rheinstahl Nord See Werke, Emden.
These submarines, projected in 1957, were the first postwar German U boats. U1 was fitted with stern torpedo tubes but paid off in 1966. U2 paid off in 1963 and U3, after three years loan to Norway, was paid off in 1967.
The "205" class was built in three groups, U4-8, U9-12, and replacements for U1 and U2 which commissioned in 1966/1967. All these and the "206" class were built of anti-magnetic steel and specially designed for operations in the Baltic. In addition two submarines of the "202" class, Hans Techel and Friedrich Schürer, were built in 1965/1966, being paid off a year later.

S172 and *S173* — Type 206

FRANCE

Type: Coastal Submarine (1)
Class: "Gustave Zedé"
Displacement, tons: 270
Dimensions, feet: 160 x 10.4 x 12
Torpedo armament: 1 tube (3 torpedoes)
Guns: 1 x 18in
Main machinery: Electric motor of 220hp; one shaft
Speed, knots: 10 surfaced; 5 dived
Complement: 8
Dates: 1893
Special features: Range – about 8 hours at 6 knots both surfaced and dived

Notes: The inception of the French Submarine Service was so marked by examples of fascinating ingenuity, flair and enthusiasm that it is extremely difficult to choose a starting point, Goubet built two craft, *Goubet II* being completed at Cherbourg in 1889, two years after her two-man prototype. These were propelled by electric motors, a principle developed in Spain by Isaac Peral in his 1886 submarine. Lacking hydroplanes they proved almost impossible to handle underwater. Where Goubet failed, Gustave Zedé succeeded with *Gymnote*, a 31-ton experimental boat which started trials in 1888. Eventually she was fitted with three pairs of hydroplanes and mounted a single 14in torpedo tube, although this was discarded in 1898. Zedé immediately started a new design after nearly two years of trials with *Gymnote* but died before seeing the result. In honour of her designer this boat received his name, being launched at Toulon in June 1893. During trials she was fitted with three sets of hydroplanes (one amidships) a casing and a bridge around her conning tower. With experience gained in her trials Romazotti (Gustave Zedé's successor) designed the "Morse" class of 146 tons which were completed in 1900-1902. These, with a surface speed of 12 knots, a periscope and two external torpedoes in slings in addition to the single tube were the first French boats really capable of any form of operations. They were named *Morse*, *Français* and *Algerien*.

Gustave Zedé (E.C.A.P.)

FRANCE

Type: Coastal Submarines (5)
Class: "Narval"
Displacement, tons: 106 surfaced; 200 dived
Dimensions, feet: 111 x 12 x 13
Torpedo armament: 4 torpedoes in external slings
Main machinery: 1 triple expansion reciprocating steam engine of 220ihp; 1 main motor of 80hp; 1 shaft
Speed, knots: 10 surfaced; 5.5 dived (*Narval*). 12/8 in later boats
Complement: 12
Dates: 1897-1901
Special features: Range 430 miles at 7 knots surfaced

Notes: This submarine *Narval* (followed closely by four boats of an improved class – *Triton, Sirene, Silure* and *Espadon*) was designed by Maxime Laubeuf, later Engineer-in-Chief to the French Navy. A radical change in external hull form resulted from her double-hull design which was totally enclosed in an external casing of comparatively normal surface-ship shape. Forward and after hydroplanes were fitted, as well as twin periscopes. The greater advance was in the fitting of steam propulsion for surface running as well as an electric motor for dived work and a generator driven by the main engine to recharge the batteries. This class had a reserve of buoyancy of 26.5%. The main disadvantage of these steam-driven boats was the 15 minutes it took to dive, mainly taken up in shutting down the boiler room and intake. This was 5 to 6 times longer than required in the all-electric submarines. The Laubeuf design had been chosen from a competition in 1896 and in 1902 a series of comparative trials was held between the Laubeuf and Romazotti designs. The outcome of these trials suggest a measure of in-fighting in the Ministry and in March 1905 a second series was undertaken between Laubeuf's design and that of Mangas. As a result 18 boats of Laubeuf's "Pluviose" class were confirmed and a further series of trials scheduled for 1908.

Espadon (E.C.A.P.)

FRANCE

Type: Coastal Submarines (33)
Class: "Pluviôse"
Displacement, tons: 391 surfaced; 550 dived
Dimensions, feet: 168 x 16.5 x 10
Torpedo armament: 6 or 7 launchers x 18in
Main machinery: Originally steam driven – later boats petrol driven – final design with heavy oil engines 800hp, main motors
Speed, knots: 12 surfaced; 9 dived
Complement: 24
Dates: 1908-1912

Notes: For reasons now unknown the French Navy ordered a number of submarines of various designs in the early 1900 s. By early 1909, apart from those already listed France operated the following:
(a) *Foller, Gnôme, Korrigan* of 182 tons completed 1903
(b) *Alose, Anguille, Bonite, Castor, Dorade, Esturgeon, Grondin, Loutre, Ludion, Lynx, Méduse, Naiade, Otarie, Oursin, Perle, Phoque, Protée, Souffleur, Thon, Truite* of 67 tons completed 1903-1905

(c) *X* and *Z* (Mangas) of 165/199 tons completed 1905
(d) *Emeraude, Opale, Rubis, Saphir, Topaze, Turquoise* (Maugas) of 390 tons completed 1903-1908
(e) *Calypso* and *Circe* (Laubeuf) of 351 tons completed 1906-1908
(f) *Aigrette, Cignone* (Laubeuf) improved "Narvals" completed 1905
(g) *Omega* of 394 tons completed 1907
(h) *Argonaute* (Bertin) of 168 tons completed 1908
There were also designs in hand by Bertin, Bourdelle, Caverley, Hutter, Radigent and Simont.
The "Pluviôse" class, of which the first 18 were laid down in August 1905, were built at three dockyards.
Cherbourg: *Brumaire, Eular, Floreal, Foucault, Franklin, Frimaire, Fructidor, Germinal, Messidor, Nivose, Pluviôse, Prairial, Thermidor, Ventose (Brumaire, Frimaire* and *Nivose* petrol driven)
Roquefort: *Berthelot, Cugnot, Faraday, Fresnel, Giffard, Montgolfier, Newton, Papin, Volta, Watt* (all heavy oil motors, except steam in *Cugnot, Giffard* and *Watt*)
Toulon: *Ampere, Arago, Bernoulli, Colomb, Curie, Gay-Lussac, Joule, Le Verrier, Monge* (all heavy oil motors)

Pluviôse (E.C.A.P.)

FRANCE

Type: Patrol Submarines (2)
Class: "Gustave Zede"
Displacement, tons: 840 surfaced; 1,098 dived
Dimensions, feet: 242.7 x 19.7 x 13.8
Torpedo armament: 2 x 18in tubes, 6 x 18in external fittings
Guns: 1 x 14pdr; 1 x 3pdr
Main machinery: 2 diesels of 1,200bhp; 2 main motors of 1,540hp; 2 shafts
Speed, knots: 16.5 surfaced; 10.5 dived
Complement: 40
Dates: 1914-1916
Special features: Range about 3,000 miles at 10 knots surfaced, 22 hours at 5 knots dived

Notes: Designed by Simonot, these two boats *(Gustave Zede and Nereide)* were built by Toulon Dockyard. Although Laubeuf had, in 1908, made a flat statement that he would not consider submarines of 700-800 tons as their large size would result in so many inherent disadvantages (*"In medio stat virtus"* was his quotation) the new *Gustave Zede* and her sister were put in the 1911 programme to be followed two years later by *Daphne* and *Diane* of about the same dimensions. They were not only the first French boats of over 1,000 tons dived displacement, but also the largest so far built in the world.

Daphne (E.C.A.P.)

FRANCE

Type: Patrol Submarines (3 + 8)
Class: "Bellone/Amarante"
Displacement, tons: 530 surfaced; 790 dived
Dimensions, feet: 196·8 x 17.7 x 12
Torpedo armament: 2 x 18in tubes (bow) + 6 dropping slings
Guns: 1 x 14pdr
Main machinery: Two diesels of 1,560hp; two main motors of 800hp; 2 shafts
Speed, knots: 15.8 surfaced; 9 dived
Complement: 29
Dates: 1914-1918
Special features: Range 1,300 miles at 12 knots surfaced, 23 hours at 5 knots dived

Notes: The above details refer to the "Bellone" class of *Bellone* (Rochefort DY); *Hermione* and *Gorgone* (Toulon DY). With the "Amarante" class comprising *Amarante*, *Arethuse*, *Artemis*, *Atalante* (Toulon DR); *Anphitrite*, *Astrée* (Rochefort DY); *Andromaque* and *Ariane* (Cherbourg DR), these were Hutter-designed boats derived from Laubeuf's "Pluviôse" class. The "Amarante" class, although ordered in the same 1912 programme as the "Bellone" class, was slightly smaller and slower. *Ariane* was lost and *Amarante* and *Astree* converted for minelaying, carrying 12 mines in place of torpedoes. The interesting point here is the length of time taken in building, the majority being completed, during the war, four years after ordering. Even longer was the building time of *Cornelie* and *Clorinde* of 540 tons dived with all-electric propulsion, designed by Radiguet in 1910 and completed in 1916-1917.

Bellone (E.C.A.P.)

FRANCE

Type: Patrol Submarines (3+3)
Class: "La Grange"/"Dupuy de Lome"
Displacement, tons: 854 surfaced; 1,291 dived
Dimensions, feet: 246 x 20.9 x 13.7
Torpedo armament: 2 x 18in tubes (bow) + 6in external cradles
Guns: 2 x 14pdr
Main machinery: 2 diesels of 1,450hp; 2 main motors of 800hp; 2 shafts
Speed, knots: 16 surfaced; 11 dived
Complement: 40
Dates: D de Lôme 1915-1916; La Grange 1914-1924
Special features: Range 1,450 miles at 14 knots surfaced, 23 hours at 5 knots dived

Notes: Both classes of Hutter design – *Dupuy de Lôme* and *Sane* both built at Toulon, where *La Grange*, *Regnoult* and *Romazzoti* were built, and *Laplace* at Rochefort. Details above of *Dupuy de Lôme*, "La Grange" class being very similar although with an increased range. At the same time *Pierre Chailley* was building at Le Havre and *Maurice Callot* at Bordeaux, France's first custom-built minelayers. Slightly shorter and fatter than the above boats *Chailley* was also the first to have a stern tube and also carried 24 mines.

La Grange (E.C.A.P.)

FRANCE

Type: Patrol Submarines (2)
Class: "Joessel"
Displacement, tons: 920 surfaced, 1,200 dived
Dimensions, feet: 242.8 x 23.4 x 14.5 *(Joessel)*
Torpedo armament: 8 x 18in tubes (4 bow, 4 external)
Guns: 2 x 14pdr
Main machinery: 2 diesels of 1,450hp; 2 main motors of 825hp; 2 shafts
Speed, knots: 16.5 surfaced; 11 dived
Complement: 47

Dates: 1917-1919
Special features: Range 4,200 miles at 10 knots surfaced, 23 hours at 5 knots dived

Notes: Although this Simonot designed class is most interesting, being the first with such an array of torpedo tubes (4 bow internal, 2 bow external and a twin, trainable mount on the after casing) and the first to have clocked over 18 knots on trials, there is no explanation for the difference of 3.7ft in the beam of the two boats. Both (*Joessel* and *Fulton*) were built by Cherbourg DY.

Joessel (E.C.A.P.)

FRANCE

Type: Patrol Submarines (12)
Class: "Ariane"
Displacement, tons: 600 surfaced; 765 dived
Dimensions, feet: 216.5 (pp) x 21 x 11.3
Torpedo armament: 7 x 21.7in tubes (2 bow 5 external) 13 torpedoes)
Guns: 1 x 3in; 2MG
Main machinery: 2 diesels of 1,250hp; 2 main motors of 1,000hp; 2 shafts
Speed, knots: 14 surfaced; 9.5 dived
Diving depth: 270ft
Complement: 41
Dates: 1925-1928
Special features: Range 2,000 miles at 10 knots surfaced, 18 hours at 5 knots dived

Notes: A class of submarine whose design and dimensions varied with the building yard.
Normand, Le Havre: *Ariane, Danae, Eurydice, Ondine*
Schneider, Chalons sur Sâone: *Circé, Calypso, Doris, Thetis*
A & C de la Loire, St. Nazaire: *Naiade, Sirène, Nymphe, Galatée*
They were the first French submarines to carry 21.7in torpedoes. At the time that these boats were building France was operating a mixed bag of ex foreign submarines – *Amazone* and *Artigone* (ex Greek), *Armide* (ex Japanese), *O'Byrne, Dupetit-Thouars* and *Henri Fournier* (ex Russian), (all the former taken over whilst building in France), plus surrendered German U-Boats *Roland Morillot* (ex UB26) *Rene Audry* (ex U119), *Victor Reveille* (ex U79) *Jean Corre* (ex UB155) *Carissan* (ex UB99), *Trinite Schillemans* (ex UB94), *Pierre Marrast* (ex U162), *Jean Roulier* (ex U166), *Halbronn* (ex U139), *Jean Autric* (ex U105), and *Leon Mignot* (ex U109)

Sirene (E.C.A.P.)

FRANCE

Type: Patrol Submarines (22)
Class: "Diane"
Displacement, tons: 558 to 662 surfaced; 800 to 858 dived
Dimensions, feet: 219.7 x 18 x 14
Torpedo armament: 8 x 21.7in tubes in first 16 boats; 7 x 21.7in tubes and 2 x 15.7in in last 6
Guns: 1 x 3in; 1 x MG
Main machinery: 2 diesels of 1,300-1,800hp; 2 main motors of 1,000hp; 2 shafts
Speed, knots: 14 surfaced, 9 dived
Complement: 48
Dates: 1929-1939
Special features: Range 3,000 miles at 10 knots surfaced, 16 hours at 5 knots dived

Notes: At last some continuity was apparent with this class, whose building was spread over six programmes.
Schneider: *Argonaute, Arethuse, Atalante, La Vestale, La Sultane*
Normand: *Diane, Méduse, Amphitrite, Orphée, La Psyché, Junon, Pallas*
Worms: *Antiope, Amazone, Oréade, La Sybille, Vénus, Cérès*
Loire: *Orion*
Dubigeon: *Ondine, Iris*
Cherbourg: *Minerve*
The last six of this class were the first to be built from Ministry of Marine designs, the first step towards standardisation.

Diane (P.A. Vicary)

FRANCE

Type: Patrol Submarines (9)
Class: "Requin"
Displacement, tons: 974 surfaced; 1,441 dived
Dimensions, feet: 257.5 (pp) x 23 x 17.8
Torpedo armament: 10 x 21.7in (4 bow, 2 stern plus 2 pairs Trainable externals in forward and after casings). 16 torpedoes – 32 in *Caiman*, *Espadon* and *Phoque*.
Guns: 1 x 3.9in; 2 MG
Main machinery: 2 diesels of 1,450hp; 2 main motors of 900hp; 2 shafts
Speed, knots: 16 surfaced; 10 dived
Diving depth: 270ft
Complement: 51

Dates: 1926-1927
Special features: Range 7,000 miles at 9 knots surfaced, 21 hours at 5 knots dived

Notes: An impressive class of submarines built under the 1922-1923 Programmes and Votes – all modernised 1935-1937. Fuzier – Roquebert design.
Cherbourg: *Requin, Morse, Narval, Souffleur, Caiman*
Toulon: *Dauphin, Espadon*
Brest: *Marsouin, Phoque*
Four *(Dauphin, Espadon, Phoque, Requin)* were seized by the Germans in Bizerta in December 1942 and turned over to the Italians. *Phoque* was subsequently sunk and the others scuttled.

Requin

FRANCE

Type: Minelaying Submarines (6)
Class: "Saphir"
Displacement, tons: 669 surfaced; 925 dived
Dimensions, feet: 216.5 x 23.7 x 16
Torpedo armament: 3 x 21.7in tubes (2 bow, 1 stern external) 5 torpedoes; 2 x 15.7in aft
Mines: 32 mines in individual chutes in ballast tanks
Guns: 1 x 3in
Main Machinery: 2 diesel engines of 1,300hp; 2 main motors of 1,000hp; 2 shafts

Speed, knots: 12 surfaced; 9 dived
Diving depth: 270ft
Complement: 42

Notes: All built at Toulon 1926-1936. *Rubis* carried out 22 minelaying patrols under the Free French ensign 1940-1945. *Saphir* and *Turquoise* were captured in Bizerta December 1942, *Le Diamant* was scuttled in Toulon 1942, *Nautilus* was sunk in Bizerta, and *Perle* operated under Free French colours. All had been deleted by 1949. Four more were never completed.

Rubis (E.C.A.P.)

FRANCE

Type: Patrol Submarines (29)
Class: "Redoubtable – 1500 tonne"
Displacement, tons: 1,380 surfaced; 2,084 dived
Dimensions, feet: 302·7 x 27 x 15.5
Torpedo armament: 9 x 21.7in tubes (4 bow, 5 external); 2 x 15.7in tubes (external aft)
Guns: 1 x 3.9in; 2MG
Main machinery: 2 diesels of 6,000hp (some 7,200, others 8,000); 2 main motors of 2,000hp; 2 shafts
Speed, knots: 17 (some 19) surfaced; 10 dived
Diving depth: 270ft
Complement: 61
Dates: 1930-1937
Special features: Range 10,000 miles at 10 knots surfaced, 20 hours at 5 knots dived

Notes: A large class of Roquebert design provided under the 1925-1930 Programmes.
Loire (Nantes): *Acheron, Actéon, Casabianca, Le Conquerant,*

Pegase, Sfax
Brest D.Y.: *Achille, Ajax, Le Centaure, Le Heros, Pascal, Pasteur*
Cherbourg D.Y.: *Agosta, Beveziers, L'Espoir, Ouessant, Sidi Ferruch, Redoubtable* (1st of class) *Vengeur, Le Glorieux*
CNF (Caen): *Archimede, Persée*
Dubigeon (Nantes): *Argo*
St.Nazaire/Penhoet: *Fresnel*
Lorient D.Y.: *Henri Poincare, Poncelet*
F. et C. de la M. (La Seyne): *Monge, Protée, Le Tonnant*
These boats had an interesting torpedo armament having external tubes in two groups. Immediately abaft the conning tower was a triple 21.7in mounting whilst in the after end of the casing they mounted a quadruple grouping of two 21.7in tubes and two 15.7in tubes. These small torpedoes had a range of only 1,500 yards. Although this was a fine class of submarine their overall record was not particularly glorious – thirteen were scuttled at various times, three sunk by RN off Diego Suarez in May 1942, two off Dakar in September 1940 and all but the six who survived sunk fairly early in the war.

Redoutable (E.C.A.P.)

FRANCE

Type: Submarine Cruiser (1)
Class: "Surcouf"
Displacement, tons: 3,250 surfaced; 4,304 dived
Dimensions, feet: 361 x 29.5 x 23.7
Torpedo armament: 8 x 21.7in tubes (4 bow, 4 external aft, 14 torpedoes); 4 x 15.7in tubes (aft, 8 torpedoes)
Guns: 2 x 8in (in turret); 2 x 37mm; 2MG
Main machinery: 2 Sulzer diesels of 7,600hp; 2 main motors of 3,400hp; 2 shafts
Speed, knots: 18.5 surfaced; 10 dived
Diving depth: 400ft (?)
Complement: 118
Dates: 1930
Special features: Range 12,000 miles at 10 knots surfaced, 12 hours at 5 knots dived

Notes: Designed by Roquebert under the 1926 Programme,

Surcouf was, in her time, the largest submarine in the world. Her vast and ponderous dimensions were necessary to carry all the items considered necessary for world-wide commerce raiding. The twin 8in turret forward of the conning tower was controlled by a director and a 40ft rangefinder. The lesser guns were mounted on the top of the small seaplane hangar which was in the tail of the conning tower. Other unusual features were a compartment for 40 prisoners, a 16ft motor cutter, a magazine for 600 rounds of 8in ammunition and extra large fuel tanks. The decision to mount such large guns with a range of 15 miles seems a little extraordinary when the director's visual horizon could not have been more than 7 miles and even then ranging must have been problematical. Presumably at greater ranges spotting by the seaplane would have been possible.

For such a large submarine her diving time of 2 minutes was good, although it took longer than this to open fire after surfacing.

By a strange fate *Surcouf* was lost when rammed accidentally by the merchant ship *Thomson Lykes* in February 1942.

Surcouf

FRANCE

Type: Patrol Submarines (7)
Class: "L'Aurore"
Displacement, tons: 893 surfaced; 1,170 dived
Dimensions, feet: 241.3 x 21.3 x 13.7
Torpedo armament: 9 x 21.7in tubes (4 bow, 3 external amidships, 2 stern externals)
Guns: 1 x 3.9in; 2MG
Main machinery: 2 diesels of 3,000hp; 2 main motors of 1,400hp; 2 shafts
Speed, knots: 14.5 surfaced; 9 dived
Diving depth: 340ft
Complement: 44
Dates: 1933-1949
Special features: Range 5,600 miles at 10 knots surfaced; 17 hours at 5 knots dived

Notes: The above details are for the original design of this, the last pre-war class. Only L'Aurore (Toulon) was completed by 1940. L'Africaine and Le Favorite (Worms) and L'Andromede (Nantes) were taken over the by Germans as UF1, 2 and 3 respectively although only UF2 was completed. After the war L'Africaine was restored to France and completed along with L'Andromede, whilst L'Artemis (Normand), L'Astrée (Nantes) and La Creole (Le Havre) were finally completed. L'Aurore was scuttled in Toulon and the remaining 8 boats planned were cancelled or dismantled. Those eventually commissioned not only appeared with many varied silhouettes but also had their surface range increased to 9,000 miles at 10 knots, their armament altered to 10 x 21.7in tubes, 1 x 3.5in and 4 x 20mm guns, and their complement increased to 63. During the war the "Phénix" class (improved "L'Aurore") and "Emeroude" class minelayers with only one laid down were cancelled.

Creole (M. Bar)

FRANCE

Type: Patrol Submarines (6)
Class: "Narval"
Displacement, tons: 1,635 surfaced; 1,910 dived
Dimensions, feet: 257 x 23.7 x 18.5
Torpedo armament: 6 x 21.7in tubes (bow – 14 reloads)
Main machinery: 2 diesels of 4,000hp; 2 main motors of 5,000hp; 2 shafts
Speed, knots: 15 surfaced; 18 dived
Diving depth: 600ft
Complement: 63
Dates: 1957-1960
Special features: Capable of 45-day patrol. Range 15,000 miles at 8 knots (snorting)

Notes: The first post-war design (with acknowledgement to the German Type 21) ordered under the 1949-1954 Programmes, Narval being laid down in 1951.
Cherbourg: *Narval, Marsouin, Dauphin, Requin*
Normand: *Espadon*
A.C.Seine: *Morse*
The whole class was modernised between 1966 and 1970, having their original Schneider diesels replaced by SEMT Pielstick engines, for diesel-electric drive as well as new weapon and detection systems. The bow sonar dome on the fore-casing was added in the mid-1950 s.
Before the "Narval" class arrived France relied on the remnants of the "L'Aurore" class, four ex-British "S" class, one ex-German Type XXI, two Type IX and two Type VIIC.

Marsouin (Wright & Logan)

FRANCE

Type: Patrol Submarines (4)
Class: "Arethuse"
Displacement, tons: 543 surfaced; 669 dived
Dimensions, feet: 162.7 x 19 x 13.1
Torpedo armament: 4 x 21.7in (bow); 4 reloads
Main machinery: SEMT Pielstick diesel electric 1,060hp/1300hp; 1 shaft
Speed, knots: 12.5 surfaced; 16 dived

Diving depth: about 600ft
Complement: 40
Dates: 1958-1960

Notes: All built at Cherbourg under 1953-1954 Programmes – *Arethuse, Argonaute, Amazone, Ariane*. Small, handy and efficient boats.

Argonaute (Wright & Logan)

FRANCE

Type: Patrol Submarines (9)
Class: "Daphne"
Displacement: 869 surfaced; 1,043 dived
Dimensions, feet: 189.6 x 22.3 x 15.1
Torpedo armament: 12 x 21.7in tubes (8 bow, 4 stern)
Main machinery: SEMT Pielstick diesel-electric 1,300hp/1,600hp; 2 shafts
Speed, knots: 13.5 surfaced; 16 dived
Diving depth: about 1,000ft
Complement: 45
Dates: 1964-1969

Special features: Range 2,700 miles at 12.5 knots surfaced; 4,500 at 5 knots (snorting)

Notes: This class is an improvement on the "Arethuse" design. The first five (*Daphne, Diane* at Dubigeon and *Doris, Flore* and *Galatée* at Cherbourg) were laid down in 1958, the later four (*Junon* and *Venus* at Cherbourg, *Psyche* and *Sirene* at Brest) in 1961. The class underwent modernisation from 1971 onwards to improve the sonar and armament. A new sonar dome is one of the outcomes.
This is a popular export model – Pakistan (3) Portugal (4), South Africa (3), Spain (built in Spain) (4).

Psyche (Wright & Logan)

FRANCE

Type: Patrol Submarines (4)
Class: "Agosta"
Displacement, tons: 1,470 surfaced; 1,790 dived
Dimensions, feet: 221.7 x 22.3 x 17.7
Torpedo armament: 4 x 21.7in tubes (20 reloads)
Main machinery: Diesel-electric; 2 SEMT Pielstick diesels of 3,600hp; 1 main motor of 4,600hp; 1 cruising motor; 1 shaft
Speed, knots: 12 surfaced; 20 dived
Complement: 50
Dates: 1976-1977
Special features: Range 9,000 miles at 9 knots (snorting) 100 hours at 3.5 knots dived

Notes: A completely new design of submarines all building at Cherbourg *(Agosta, Beveziers, La Praya, Ouessant), Agosta* being laid down in February 1972 for trials in November 1974.
Late in 1973 it was announced that a nuclear-propelled Fleet-Submarine programme would be started in the 1974 Budget. This is to be a single-reactor, single-screw boat of about 2,500 tons with a speed of 25 knots plus to be laid down in 1976. Two squadrons of this class are forecast, one to be stationed at Brest and one at Toulon.

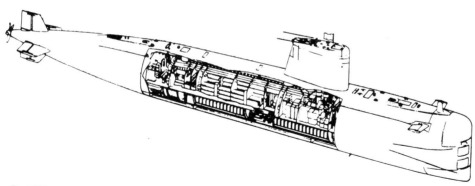

Beveziers

FRANCE

Type: Ballistic Missile Submarines (6)
Class: "Le Redoubtable"
Displacement, tons: 7,500 surfaced; 9,000 dived
Dimensions, feet: 420 x 34.8 x 32.8
Missile armament: 16 tubes for MSBS
Torpedo armament: 4 x 21.7in tubes (bow – 18 torpedoes)
Main machinery: Pressurised water-cooled nuclear reactor; 2 turbines 15,000shp; 2 turbo-alternators; 1 shaft
Speed, knots: 20 surfaced; 25 dived
Diving depth: 700ft plus
Complement: 135 (2 crews)
Dates: 1971-1978

Special features: 1 auxiliary diesel with a range of 5,000 miles

Notes: These six SSBN s(*Le Redoubtable, Le Terrible, Le Foudroyant, L'Indomptable, Le Tonnant, L'Inflexible*) have been built or are building at Cherbourg, the first being laid down in 1964. The first boats were armed with MSBS1 with a Rita 1 motor and a range of 1,350 miles. MSBS2 is now (1976) in production with a Rita II motor and a range out to 1,620 miles. By 1976 the M-20 (M2 with a thermonuclear head) is expected, and by the late 1970s the M3 or M4 may carry MRV/MIRV to a range of 3,000 miles.
Gymnote, a conversion from an unused diesel-propelled hull, was completed in 1966 for test-firing of these missiles.

Le Redoutable, Le Terrible & Le Foudroyant (E.C.A.P.)

Holland No. 1

Holland No. 6

JAPAN

Type: Coastal Submarines (5)
Class: "Holland"
Displacement, tons: 105 surfaced; 730 dived
Dimensions, feet: 65 x 11.7 x 10.3
Torpedo armament: 1 x 18in (bow – 2 torpedoes)
Main machinery: 1 petrol engine, 180hp; 1 main motor 70hp; 1 shaft
Speed, knots: 9 surfaced; 7 dived
Complement: 13
Dates: 1905
Special features: Range 190 miles surfaced at 8 knots

Notes: The Japanese were slow to take an interest in submarines but after the Russian war of 1904 they took swift action, ordering *Holland 1-5* from Fore River Yard, Quincy, U.S.A. These were shipped to Yokohama and reassembled, remaining in service until 1922.
At the same time as these operational boats were building two more, *6* and *7*, were under construction by Kawasaki. These were much smaller experimental boats of 65 and 95 tons dived displacement with a single 18in tube and no reload.

JAPAN

Type: Coastal Submarines (5)
Class: "Vickers C1" and "C2"
Displacement, tons: 286/321 (C1); 291/326 (C2)
Dimensions, feet: 142 x 13.5 x 11.3
Torpedo armament: 2 x 18in tubes (bow – no reloads)
Main machinery: One petrol engine of 600hp; one main motor of 300hp; 1 shaft
Speed, knots: 12 surfaced; 8.5 dived
Complement: 16
Dates: 1909-1911
Special features: Range 650 miles at 12 knots, surfaced 15 hours at 4 knots dived

Notes: These boats (Nos. 8-12) were generally similar to the British "C" class although the range was slightly less. Built at Barrow by Vickers-Armstrong and shipped to Japan for re-assembly at Kure. All were renumbered in 1924, Ha 1-5 being disposed of in 1929. Kawasaki again built a Japanese version of the foreign imports, No. 13. She was basically similar to the Vickers design but with double the surface horsepower, giving an extra 2 knots. Renumbered Ha6 in 1924.

No. 10 ("Vickers C" type)

JAPAN

Type: Patrol Submarines (2)
Class: "Type S" (14-15); "S2" (14ii)
Displacement, tons: 457 surfaced; 665 dived
Dimensions, feet: 186.3 x 17 x 9.7
Torpedo armament: 6 x 18in tubes (2 bow, 4 external. 8 torpedoes)
Guns: 1 MG
Main machinery: 2 diesels of 2,000hp; 2 main motors of 800hp
Speed, knots: 17 surfaced, 10 dived
Dates: 1916-1917
Special features: Range 2,000 miles at 10 knots surfaced, 15 hours at 4 knots dived

Notes: These two boats were ordered from Creusot to a Schneider-Laubeuf design but only No.15 (renumbered Ha10 in 1924) reached Japan, No.14 being taken over by the French as *Armide* in 1916. In 1918 a second No.14 of basically the same design was laid down at Kure, becoming Ha9 in 1924.
Under the pressure of war it was decided to build at home and in 11 months in 1916 Nos. 16 and 17 (Vickers type) were built at Kure. They were much the same as the original Vickers boats, reverting to 600hp engines but mounting four extra external tubes with a total of eight torpedoes carried. Renumbered Ha7 and 8 in 1924.

"Type S" No. 15

JAPAN

Type: Patrol Submarines (2+3)
Class: "F1"-"F2" (18 and 21, 31-33)
Displacement, tons: 717 surfaced; 1,047 dived
Dimensions, feet: 215·3 x 20 x 13.7
Torpedo armament: 5 x 18in tubes (3 bow, 2 stern. 8 torpedoes)
Guns: 1 x 3in fitted in 1922
Main machinery: 2 diesels of 2,500bhp; 2 main motors of 1,200shp; 2 shafts
Speed, knots: 17 surfaced; 8 dived ("F2" 18 surfaced)
Complement: 40
Dates: "F1" 1921 "F2" 1922
Special features: Range 3,500 miles at 10 knots surfaced; 20 hours at 4 knots dived

Notes: Further desire for experiments led to these boats of Fiat-Laurenti design – 18 of the 1915-1916 Programme, 21 of 1916-1917, 31-33 of 1918-1919. The "F2" was a slight modification of "F1" all being built by Kawasaki yard, Kobe to Italian plans. Renumbered RO 1-5 in sequence in 1924.
With a range almost double that of their longest-range predecessors and with heavier scantlings than originally designed these boats were much more suitable for operations in the North-West Pacific.

RO 2 — Type F1 (Anthony J. Watts Collection)
RO 5 — Type F2 (Anthony J. Watts Collection)

JAPAN

Type: Patrol Submarines (2+3)
Class: "K1" and "K2"
Displacement, tons: 735 surfaced; 1,030 dived
Dimensions, feet: 227 x 20.7 x 11.3
Torpedo armament: 6 x 18in tubes (4 bow, 2 stern. 10 torpedoes)
Guns: 1 x 3in; 1 MG
Main machinery: 2 diesels of 2,600bhp; 2 main motors of 1,200 shp; 2 shafts
Speed, knots: 18 surfaced; 9 dived
Complement: 40
Dates: 1919
Special features: Range 4,000 miles at 10 knots surfaced; 21 hours at 4 knots dived

Notes: These two boats (No. 19 and 20) were built by Kure Naval Yard, their design being a Japanese adaptation of the Schneider-Laubeuf type used for No. 15. They were the largest so far built for the Imperial Navy and of rugged construction to cope with local conditions.

In 1918 Japan acquired six German U boats which were in service for approximately three years.

The "K1" class (1916 programme) was sufficiently successful for the three boats (22,23,24) of the "K2" class to be ordered under the 1917 programme. These were virtually the same as their predecessors with the range increased to 6,000 miles. Renumbered in 1924 as follows: 19, RO 4; 20 RO 12; 22-24 RO 13-15.

RO 14 — Type K2 (Anthony J. Watts Collection)
RO 11 — Type K1 (Anthony J. Watts Collection)

JAPAN

Type: Patrol Submarines (2+4+3)
Class: "L1", "L2", and "L3"
Displacement, tons: 902 surfaced; 1,195 dived
Dimensions, feet: 231.5 x 23.5 x 12.7
Torpedo armament: 4 or 6 x 18in tubes (4 bow, 2 beam external in 25 and 26 only – 10 torpedoes)
Guns: 1 x 3in; 1 MG
Main machinery: 2 diesels of 2,400bhp;. 2 main motors of 1,600shp; 2 shafts
Speed, knots: 17 surfaced; 8 dived

Complement: 48
Dates: 1920-1923
Special features: Range 5,500 miles at 10 knots surfaced; 20 hours at 4 knots dived

Notes: All built by Mitsubishi, Kobe to British Vickers design similar to the RN "L" class submarines. "L1" included 25 and 26, "L2" 27-30 and "L3" 46, 47 and 57. All renumbered in 1924 as RO 51-59. In 25 and 26 the two external torpedo tubes were amidships beam tubes. The "L3" class survived the war and was scrapped in 1946.

RO 58 — Type L3 (Anthony J. Watts Collection)

JAPAN

Type: Patrol Submarines (10+3)
Class: "K3" and "K4"
Displacement, tons: "K3": 755/1,050; "K4": 770/1,070
Dimensions, feet: "K3": 230 x 20 x 12.3; "K4": 243 x 20 x 12.3
Torpedo armament: "K3": 6 x 18in (4 bow, 2 beam. 10 torpedoes); "K4": 4 x 21in (bow. 8 torpedoes)
Guns: 1 x 3in; 1 MG
Main machinery: 2 diesels of 2,600bhp; 2 main motors of 1,200shp; 2 shafts
Speed, knots: "K3" 17/8; "K4" 16/8
Complement: 45

Dates: 1922-1924
Special features: Range 6,000 at 10 knots surfaced, 21 hours at 4 knots dived

Notes: These two classes were improvements on the "K2" class and were the first standard design to appear in the Japanese Navy. The "K3"s were ordered under the 1918 programme and the "K4"s under the 1919-1921 programmes, the use of 21in torpedoes dating from the 1919 programme. Renumbered in 1924 RO 16-28 in sequence of original numbers 34-43 ("K3") and 45, 58 and 42 ("K4").

RO 16 — Type K3 (Anthony J. Watts Collection)

JAPAN

Type: Cruiser Submarines (1 + 1)
Class: "KD1" and "KD2"
Displacement, tons: 1,500 surfaced; 2,430 dived
Dimensions, feet: "KD1": 300 x 29 x 15; "KD2": 330 x 25 x 17
Torpedo armament: 8 x 21in tubes (4 bow, 2 stern. 24 torpedoes in "KD1", 16 in "KD2")
Guns: 1 x 4.7, 1 x 3in
Main machinery: "KD1": 4 diesels of 5,200bhp; 2 main motors of 2,000shp; 4 shafts. "KD2": 2 diesels of 6,800bhp; 2 main motors of 2,000shp; 2 shafts
Speed, knots: "KD1" 20 surfaced; "KD2" 21 surfaced
Complement: 60
Dates: 1924-1925
Special features: Range "KD1": 20,000 miles at 10 knots surfaced, 25 hours at 4 knots dived. "KD2": 10,000 miles at 10 knots surfaced, 25 hours at 4 knots dived

Notes: These two submarines (44-"KD1", 51-"KD2") were the result of the Japanese following the Western trail of overgrown submarines. The "KD2" class was larger but carried less oil fuel than the "KD1", resulting in a halving of the surface range.
"KD2"'s original machinery layout with four shafts not surprisingly proved unsatisfactory and shortly after completion two diesels and two shafts were removed.
The "KD2" class was based on the German U139, causing the differences between the classes including the reduction to only 16 torpedoes. The requirements of the Washington Treaty came into force at about this time and resulted in the cancellation of orders for 17 different submarines. Renumbered as follows, No.44 to 151 in 1924 and No.51 to I52 in 1924 and I152 in 1942.

I152 — Type KD2 (Anthony J. Watts Collection)

JAPAN

Type: Patrol Submarines (9)
Class: "L4"
Displacement, tons: 996 surfaced; 1,322 dived
Dimensions, feet: 250 x 24.3 x 12.3
Torpedo armament: 6 x 21in tubes (bow) (10 torpedoes)
Guns: 1 x 3in; 1 MG
Main machinery: 2 diesels of 2,400bhp; 2 main motors of 1,600shp; 2 shafts
Speed, knots: 16 surfaced; 8 dived
Complement: 48

Dates: 1923-1927
Special features: Range 5,500 miles at 10 knots surfaced, 20 hours at 4 knots dived

Notes: This class (Nos. 59, 72,73,84, RO 64-68) was the last in the Japanese Navy built to British design. The 3in gun was moved from the conning tower ("L3" class) and mounted on the fore-casing. No stern tubes fitted. Renumbered as follows in 1924 – 59,72,73,84 to RO 60-63. All built by Mitsubishi, Kobe.

RO 64 — Type L4 (Anthony J. Watts Collection)

JAPAN

Type: Patrol Submarines (4)
Class: "KT"
Displacement, tons: 665 surfaced; 1,000 dived
Dimensions, feet: 243.5 x 20 x 12.3
Torpedo armament: 4 x 21in tubes (bow) (8 torpedoes)
Guns: 1 x 4.7in; 1 MG
Main machinery: 2 diesels of 1,200bhp; 2 main motors of 1,200shp; 2 shafts
Speed, knots: 13 surfaced; 8 dived
Complement: 43

Dates: 1923-1927
Special features: Range 6,000 miles at 10 knots surfaced, 21 hours at 4 knots dived

Notes: This class was designed by the Japanese Navy and built by Kawasaki Kobe (68-71 renumbered RO 29-32 in 1924). The engines were Fiats of less than half the horsepower in the "K4" class, resulting in a drop of 3 knots in surface speed. This was the first of the smaller classes to mount a 4.7in gun.

RO 30, No. 69 — Type KT (U.S. Bureau of Ships)

JAPAN

Type: Submarine Cruisers (4+1+1)
Class: "J1", "J1M", "J2"
Displacement, tons: "J1" 2135/2791; "J1M" 2243/2921; "J2" 2243/3061
Dimensions, feet: "J1" and "J1M": 320 x 30.3 x 16.5; "J2": 323 x 29.7 x 17.5
Torpedo armament: 6 x 21in tubes (4 bow, 2 stern). 20 torpedoes in "J1" and "J1M". 17 in "J2"
Guns: 2 x 5.5in in "J1" and "J1M", 1 x 5in and 1 x 13mm in "J2"
Main machinery: 2 diesels of 6,000bhp in "J1" and "J1M"; 8,000 in "J2"; 2 main motors of 2,600shp; 2 shafts
Speed, knots: "J1" and "J1M" 18 surfaced; 8 dived
Diving depth: 260ft
Complement: 68
Dates: 1926-1935
Special features: Range 24,000 at 10 knots surfaced (20,000 in "J2") 20 hours at 3 knots dived

Notes: These three classes ("J1",-74,75,76,14; "J1M",-15; "J2",-16) were all built by Kawasaki Kobe. 74-76 renumbered I1-I3 in 1924. These were designed as long-range marauders, I1 carrying out a trial cruise of 25,000 miles within her provision limit of 60 days. They were also the deepest diving boats yet built.
15 was of similar design but included a seaplane in her armament. This was stowed in sections and assembled on the surface, a long-winded operation which resulted in its being discarded in 1940.
"J2" also had a seaplane with a catapult fitted abaft the conning tower. I1 and I2, the survivors of their class, were converted in 1942 for stores transport using the upper deck. In this guise, and not surprisingly, they were sunk.

I1 — Type J1 (Anthony J. Watts Collection)

JAPAN

Type: Submarine minelayers (4)
Class: "KRS"
Displacement, tons: 1,383 surfaced; 1,768 dived
Dimensions, feet: 279.5 x 24.5 x 14.5
Torpedo armament: 4 x 21in tubes (bow. 12 torpedoes)
Mines: 42
Guns: 1 x 5.5in
Main machinery: 2 diesels of 2,400bhp; 2 main motors of 1,100shp; 2 shafts
Speed, knots: 14.5 surfaced; 7 dived
Diving depth: 200ft
Dates: 1927-1928

Special features: Range 10,500 miles at 8 knots surfaced, 12 hours at 4 knots dived

Notes: This class (Nos. 48,49,50, and 124) was designed under the 1919 Programme and were the only minelaying submarines ever built by the Japanese.
They were built on the same plan as the German "UE" class, being constructed partly at Kawasaki Kobe and completed at Kure. Renumbered as 121-23 in 1924 and all four as I121-124 in 1939.
During the war they were all converted to act as seaplane refuellers with petrol tanks fitted on the casing.

I22 — Type KRS (Anthony J. Watts Collection)

JAPAN

Type: Patrol Submarines (9+3+3+8+6)
Class: "KD3", "4", "5", "6", "7"
Displacement, tons: "KD3","4""5"-1,750/2,300; "KD6" 1,785/2,440; "KD7" 1,833/2602
Dimensions, feet: "KD3" 330 x 25.5 x 15.7; "KD4" 320 x 25.5 x 15.7; "KD5" 320 x 26.7 x 15.5; "KD6" 244 x 27 x 15
Torpedo armament: "KD3" 8 x 21in tubes (6 bow, 2 stern. 16 torpedoes); "KD4"-"7" 6 x 21in tubes (4 bow, 2 stern. 14 torpedoes, 12 in "KD7")
Guns: 1 x 4.7in ("KD3","4" some of "6" and "7"); 1 x 3.9in ("KD5", some of "6")
Main machinery: 2 diesels "KD3". 6,800, "KD4" 6,000, "KD5" 6,000, "KD6" 9,000 "KD7" 8,000; 2 main motors of 1,800shp; 2 shafts
Speed, knots: 20/8 in "KD3"-"5", 23/8 in "KD6"-"7"
Diving depth: 200ft (250 in "KD5", "6" and "7")

Complement: 61
Dates: 1927-1943
Special features: Range at 10 knots surfaced "KD3"-"5" 10,000 miles, "KD6" 14,000 miles, "KD7" 15,000 miles. At 3 knots dived 30 hours in earlier boats, 20 hours in later

Notes: This series of large patrol submarines was designed by the Japanese Navy and built at Kure, Kobe, Sasebo and Yokohama. ("KD3"A and B64, 77 and 78 (renumbered 153-55 in 1924) 156-63, "KD4" 161, 62 and 64, "KD5" 165-67, "KD6"A and B 168-75, "KD7" 176-81). Further renumbering took place in 1942. These boats were busily engaged during the war although, towards its end, many were employed as transports for Kaiten midget submarines and, in some cases, small landing craft. It is sad to see such mis-employment of what were good submarines.

I61 — Type KD4 (A.P.)

JAPAN

Type: Patrol Submarines (2 + 18)
Class: "K5", "K6"
Displacement, tons: "K5" 940/1,350; "K6" 115/1,447
Dimensions, feet: "K5", 240 x 22 x 10½; "K6" 264 x 23 x 13.3
Torpedo armament: 4 x 21in tubes (bow. 10 torpedoes)
Guns: 1 x 3in; 1 x 13mm ("K5") 2 x 25mm ("K6")
Main machinery: Two diesels of 3,000bhp in "K5" and 4,200 in "K6"; 2 main motors of 1,200shp; 2 shafts
Speed, knots: 19/20 surfaced; 8 dived
Diving depth: 250/260ft
Complement: 62
Dates: "K5" 1935-37, "K6" 1943-1944

Special features: Range "K5" 8,000 miles at 12 knots surfaced; "K6" 11,000 miles at 12 knots surfaced. 20 hours at 4 knots dived

Notes: The "K5" class was designed as a prototype for wartime mass-production, being included in the 1931 Programme (RO 33 and 34). A little larger than the "K4" class but with increased engine power they had an extra 3 knots on their surface speed. In 1940-1941 the "K6" class (RO 35-56, RO70-99 and RO 200-227 plus nine unnumbered) was ordered. This was an improvement on the "K5" with greater speed, range and diving depth but eventually RO 51-54 and all from RO 70 onwards were overtaken by the war's changed needs and cancelled.

RO 35 — Type K-6 (A. Nani)

JAPAN

Type: Patrol Submarines (2+3+1+2)
Class: "J3", "A1", "A2", "AM"
Displacement, tons: "J3" 2,525/3,588; "A1" 2,919/4,149; "A2" 2,934/4,172; "AM" 3,603/4,762
Dimensions, feet: "J3" 323 x 29.7 x 17.5; "A1" and "2" 372.7 x 31.3 x 17.5; "AM" 372.7 x 38.5 x 19.3
Torpedo armament: 6 x 21in tubes (bow. 18 torpedoes)
Guns: "J3" 2 x 5.5in; 5 MG. Remainder 1 x 5.5in 4-7 x 25mm
Main machinery: 2 diesels "J3" 5,600bhp, "A1" 6,200bhp, "A2" 2,350bhp, "AM" 4,400bhp; 2 main motors "J3" 1,400shp, "A1" and "2" 1,200shp, "AM" 600 shp; 2 shafts
Speed, knots: "J3", "A1"-23 surfaced, 8 dived; "A2"-18 surfaced, 6 dived; "AM" 16.7 surfaced, 5.5 dived
Diving depth: 330ft
Complement: 80/100/100/108
Dates: 1937-1945
Special features: Range surface "J3" 14,000 at 16 knots, "A1" 16,000 at 16 knots, "A2" and "AM" 21,000 at 16 knots. Range dived 20/30/25/20 hours at 3 knots. Seaplanes carried "J3", 1; "A1".1; "A2".1; "AM".2

Notes: These overgrown monsters were started by "J3" class (17,18 renumbered I17 and I18) which were laid down in 1934. In 1938 19,10 and 11 were ordered to an improvement of the "J3" design – they were intended as command boats for submarine groups and were built with increased W/T facilities, a larger complement and a 90 day endurance. The "J3" class had its hangar abaft the conning tower – in subsequent classes this was reversed exchanging places with the gun. I12 (the only "A2" class boat) was very similar to the "A1" but had less engine power and greater range. The final design in this group of mammoths was the "AM" class designed to replace the outer pickets of a fleet and provided with two seaplanes. The enlarged hangar caused the bridge to be offset to port. Only two (I13 and 14) were completed. The "AM" design included an attempt at a snort mast which was a failure.

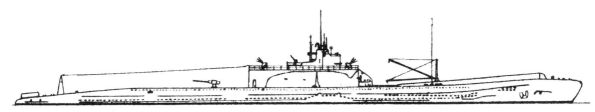

I14 — Type AM (A. Nani)

JAPAN

Type: Patrol Submarines (20+6+3)
Class: "B1", "B2" "B3"
Displacement, tons: 2,590 surfaced; 3,660 dived
Dimensions, feet: 356.5 x 30.5 x 17
Torpedo armament: 6 x 21in tubes (bow. 17 torpedoes, 19 in "B3")
Guns: 1 x 5.5in; 2 x 25mm
Main machinery: 2 diesels of 6,200bhp, (4,700 in "B3"); 2 main motors of 2,000shp (1,200in "B3"); 2 shafts
Speed, knots: 23.5 surfaced; 8 dived (17.5/6.5 in "B3")
Diving depth: 330ft
Complement: 94
Dates: 1940-1944
Special features: Range surface "B1" and "2" 14,000 miles at 16 knots. "B3" 21,000 at 16 knots. Dived "B1" and "2" 32 hours and "B3" 35 hours at 3 knots. One seaplane carried – catapult fitted

Notes: In the late 1930 s "Design for design's sake" seems to have been the motto in the Japanese Navy Ministry. The "B1" class ordered in 1937 was slightly smaller than "A1" with reduced range, same main engines, stores and armaments, and with the hangar and catapult on the forecasing. Of the "B1" class (I15,17,19,21,23,25-39) "B2" class (I40-45 with 8 more cancelled) "B3" class (I54,56,58 with 35 more cancelled) a total of 29 submarines only two survived to be surrendered – maybe a proof of the vulnerability of the very large, comparatively slow submarine. "B1" and "B2" were similar but "B3" was rendered even more vulnerable by an all-round reduction in hp. Later in the war various alterations were made to certain boats, some having the hangar replaced by another 5.1in gun, others having their guns removed to carry up to six "Kaiten" midget submarines on the casing. By 1941 an early form of radar was mounted on the hangars of these boats.

I54 — Type B3 (S. Fukui)

JAPAN

Type: Patrol Submarines (5+3+3)
Class: "C1", "C2", "C3"
Displacement, tons: 2,560 surfaced; 3,560 dived
Dimensions, feet: 358.5 x 30 x 17.5
Torpedo armament: 8 x 21in tubes (6 in "C3") 20/19 torpedoes
Guns: 1 x 5.5in; 2 x 25mm
Main machinery: 2 diesels of 6,200hp, (4,700 in "C3"); 2 main motors of 1,000shp (600 in "C3")
Speed, knots: 23.5 surfaced; 8 dived ("C3". 17.5/6.5)
Diving depth: 330ft
Complement: 95
Dates: 1940-1944
Special features: Range "C1" and "2" 14,000 miles at 16 knots surfaced, 20 hours at 3 knots dived. "C3" 21,000 miles at 16 knots surfaced, 36 hours at 3 knots dived

Notes: In 1937 the first of the "C1" class was ordered, almost identical to "B1" but without any aircraft. It is said that "A1" was designed as a command submarine, "B1" as a scouting submarine and "C1" as an attack submarine. This is probably true and such a plan shows a fundamental failure to grasp the principles of submarine warfare based on versatility, which failure was reflected in the lack of success of Japanese submarines in World War II. "C1" class (I16,18,20,22, 24) "C2" class (I46-48 with 7 more cancelled) and "C3" class (I52,53,55 with 42 more cancelled) suffered heavily, only 2 out of 11 surviving to surrender in 1945. A number were converted for carriage of "Kaiten" midget submarines.

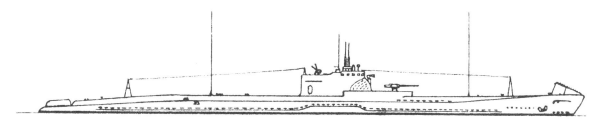

I46 — Type C2 (A. Watts)

JAPAN

Type: Patrol Submarines (18)
Class: "KS"
Displacement, tons: 601 surfaced; 785 dived
Dimensions, feet: 200 x 19.5 x 11.5
Torpedo armament: 4 x 21in tubes (8 torpedoes)
Guns: 1 x 3in
Main machinery: 2 diesels of 100bhp; 2 main motors of 750shp; 2 shafts
Speed, knots: 14.5 surfaced; 8 dived
Diving depth: 250ft
Complement: 38
Dates: 1942-1944
Special features: Range surface 3,500 miles at 12 knots, dived 20 hours at 3 knots

Notes: This class (RO 100-117, 9 more cancelled) was designed for coastal patrol, all 18 boats being sunk during the war. Some achieved comparatively long-range patrols but were inhibited in any major operations far from base, carrying only four reload torpedoes.

RO 109 — Type KS (Anthony J. Watts Collection)

JAPAN

Type: Transport Submarines (12+1)
Class: "D1" "D2"
Displacement, tons: "D1" 1,780/2,215; "D2" 1,930/2,240
Dimensions, feet: "D1" 248 x 29.3 x 15.5; "D2" 243 x 29.3 x 16.5
Guns: 1 x 5.5in; 2 x 25mm
Main machinery: 2 diesels of 1,850bhp; 2 electric motors of 1,200shp; 2 shafts
Speed, knots: 13 surfaced; 6.5 dived
Diving depth: 250ft
Complement: 60
Dates: 1944-1945
Special features: Range surfaced 15,000 miles at 10 knots, 38 hours at 3 knots dived

Notes: After about a year of hostilities it was decided in late 1942 that submarines were better fitted to supply island garrisons than were surface ships. Thus the "D1" class (I361-372 with many more planned) and "D2" class (of which only I373 was completed although another 150 were projected) were designed to carry 85 tons of stores and over 100 men with two small craft to land them. Originally two external torpedo tubes were fitted but were removed to improve seaworthiness. The main gun was mounted on the fore-casing and the single 25mm guns on the after. Most of these boats were sunk during the war, several being torpedoed on the surface by Allied submarines.

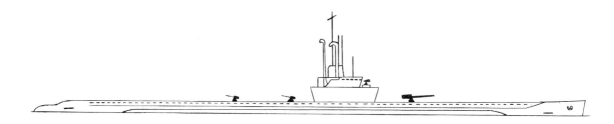

I361 — Type D1 (A. Watts)

JAPAN

Type: Supply Submarines (1+1)
Class: "SH"
Displacement, tons: 3,510 surfaced; 4,300 dived
Dimensions, feet: 364 x 33.5 x 20
Torpedo armament: 4 x 21in tubes (no reloads)
Guns: 7 x 25mm; 4 mortars
Main machinery: 2 diesels of 3,700bhp; 2 main motors of 1,200shp; 2 shafts
Speed, knots: 16 surfaced; 6 dived
Diving speed: 300ft
Complement: 77
Dates: 1945

Special features: Range surfaced 13,000 miles at 14 knots, 35 hours at 3 knots dived

Notes: This is probably the most astounding brand of submarine ever built – a mobile seaplane station. Designed to provide a supply base for floatplanes and flying boats in forward areas these monsters carried 400 tons of air stores of which 370 were fuel, 20 bombs and torpedoes and 10 fresh water. In addition space was available for a dozen aircrew. Only I351 was completed, being sunk six months after commissioning. The second was sunk in Kure DY before completion and four others were cancelled.

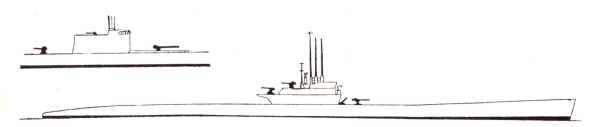

I351 — Type SH — showing alternative conning tower (A. Watts)

JAPAN

Type: Submarine Cruisers (3)
Class: "STO"
Displacement, tons: 5,225 surfaced; 6,560 dived
Dimensions, feet: 400 x 39.3 x 23
Torpedo armament: 8 x 21in tubes (20 torpedoes)
Guns: 1 x 5.5in; 10 x 25mm
Main machinery: 4 diesels of 7,700bhp; 2 main motors of 1,200shp; 2 shafts
Speed, knots: 19 surfaced; 6.5 dived
Diving depth: 330ft
Complement: 144
Dates: 1944-1945
Special features: Range surface 37,500 miles at 14 knots, 20 hours at 3 knots

Notes: These huge submarines were ordered in the 1942 Programme, being a combination of the "A", "B" and "C" classes. With twin hulls placed horizontally alongside each other and four diesels to drive them, they had an enormous casing and bridge structure with a form of snort-mast, radar, three triple 25mm and one single, the 5.5in gun being set into the after casing. As one of the roles for this class was aerial attack on shore targets (including, it is said, the Panama Canal) their design was modified to include hangar space for three seaplanes and their weapons (torpedoes and bombs), the catapult running up the fore-casing. The close interest taken by Admiral Yamamato in this and previous classes of monster suggests that this mis-application of submarine capabilities came as much from the top as anywhere. In fact only I400-402 were completed, fifteen being cancelled.

I400 — Type STO (U.S. Navy)

JAPAN

Type: Patrol submarines (3)
Class "ST"
Displacement, tons: 1,290 surfaced; 1,450 dived
Dimensions, feet: 260 x 19 x 18
Torpedo armament: 4 x 21in tubes (10 torpedoes)
Guns: 2 x 25mm (retracting into casing)
Main machinery: 2 diesels of 2,750bhp; 2 main motors of 5,000shp; 2 shafts
Speed, knots: 16 surfaced; 19 dived
Diving depth: 360ft
Complement: 30
Dates: 1945
Special features: Range surface 6,000 miles at 14 knots, dived 45 hours at 3 knots
Notes: At last the Japanese Navy produced a really efficient submarine – whereas up to date they had the doubtful distinction of producing the world's largest submarine, now they produced the fastest (19 knots for an hour). This was achieved by producing a design of reasonable displacement with a well-streamlined hull form, light-weight MAN diesels and main-motors of a hitherto unprecedented power. They were built at the same time as the German "Type XXI", maybe as the result of consultation. They were slightly smaller with the same SHP in their motors and also had extra battery sections and capacity. These two classes were the first operational submarines in history to achieve such underwater performance, although twenty-seven years before the British "R" class had shown the way which nobody, including their own navy, had chosen to follow until in 1937, the Japanese laid down Submarine No.71. This was an experimental boat of only 240 tons dived displacement which, with low-powered diesels and a fully streamlined hull, was a pig on the surface but achieved 22 knots dived. She was scrapped in 1940 after two years trials and it is extraordinary that it was four years before the lessons learned were applied to an operational design. In fact only three of the "ST" class (I201-203) were completed, 100 others being scrapped or cancelled.

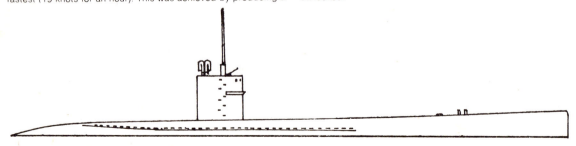

I 201 — Type ST (Anthony J. Watts Collection)

JAPAN

Type: Coastal Submarines (10)
Class: "STS" and "SS"
Displacement, tons: 430 tons surfaced; 495 dived
Dimensions, feet: 174 x 13 x 11
Torpedo armament: 2 x 21in tubes (4 torpedoes)
Guns: 1 MG
Main machinery: 1 diesel of 400bhp; 1 main motor of 1,250shp; 1 shaft
Speed, knots: 10 surfaced; 13 dived
Diving depth: 350ft
Complement: 22
Dates: 1945
Special features: Range surfaced 4,000 miles at 10 knots, dived 40 hours at 3 knots

Notes: This smaller version of the "ST" class was designed to meet the home-defence requirement in the closing years of World War II. Planned for mass production, the first was completed in two months. Despite this only ten (Ha 201-205, 207-210, 216) were finished, another 80 being scrapped or cancelled.
At about the same time as the "STS" class was in production the "SS" class was building at Senshu and Kobe (Ha 101-111, with another 90 cancelled or scrapped). This was an unarmed supply-submarine class of 500 tons dived displacement designed to carry 60 tons of stores on coastal trips and was the last class in production before the war ended.

Ha 202 — Type STS (Anthony J. Watts Collection)

JAPAN

Type: Patrol Submarines (1+4)
Class: "Oyashio" and "Hayashio"
Displacement, tons: 750/780 standard
Dimensions, feet: 193.6/200.1 x 21.3 x 13.5
Torpedo armament: 3 x 21in tubes (bow)
Main machinery: 2 diesels of 900bhp; 2 main motors of 2,300shp
Speed, knots: 11 surfaced; 15 dived
Complement: 40
Dates: 1962-1963

Notes: All details above for "Hayashio" class, the first figures being for *Hayashio* and *Wakashio* the second for *Natashio* and *Fuyushio*.
Oyashio built by Kawasaki, Kobe was the first post-war Japanese submarine. She was of 1,420 tons dived displacement with a surface speed of 13 knots and 19 knots dived, four 21in torpedo tubes and, in many ways, resembled the "ST" class of 1945. Completed in June 1960.

Oyashio

JAPAN

Type: Patrol Submarines (5)
Class: "Ooshio"
Displacement, tons: 1,650 standard
Dimensions, feet: 288.7 x 26.9 x 16.2
Torpedo armament: 8 x 21in tubes (6 bow, 2 stern)
Main machinery: 2 diesels of 2,900bhp; 2 main motors of 6,300shp; 2 shafts
Speed, knots: 14 surfaced; 18 dived
Diving depth: 600ft (?)

Complement: 80
Dates: 1965-1969

Notes: Once again Japan turned to a larger class to cope with the heavy weather off their coasts and to make use of the deep water close to. This is a class of double-hulled boats with improved sonar and a good torpedo armament. (All the class *Arashio, Asashio, Harushio, Michishio,* and *Ooshio*) were built at Kobe, 2 by Kawasaki and 3 by Mitsubishi.

Michishio

JAPAN

Type: Patrol Submarines (5+2)
Class: "Uzushio"
Displacement, tons: 1,850 standard
Dimensions, feet: 236.2 x 32.5 x 24.6
Torpedo armament: 6 x 21in tubes (bow)
Main machinery: 2 diesels of 3,400hp; 1 main motor of 7,200hp; 1 shaft
Speed, knots: 12 surfaced; 20 dived
Diving depth: 600ft (?)

Complement: 80
Dates: 1971-1977

Notes: This was a departure from the traditional hull form. With a beam-length ratio of 7.6 this class was very near to the original Albacore hull and is now the standard for new building programmes. So far *Uzushio*, *Makishio*, *Isoshio*, *Narushio* and *Kuroshio* are completed with *Takashio* and 1 other unnamed due for completion 1976-1977.

Narushio (Japanese Maritime Self-Defence Force)

U.S.S.R.

Type: Coastal Submarines (6)
Class: "Early Russian" ("Protector")
Displacement, tons: 135 surfaced; 175 dived
Torpedo armament: 3 tubes
Main machinery: 2 petrol motors; 2 electric motors; 2 shafts
Speed, knots: 10 surfaced; 7 dived
Complement: 6
Dates: 1901-1906
Special features: Fitted with wheels

Notes: The Russian interest in submarines dated back to Peter the Great who, in one of his few failures, ordered a submarine in 1729. In 1856 they paid Bauer to build a submarine in Kronstadt and in 1879 ordered thirty useless pedal-operated boats from Drzewiecki. After plans to buy an improved Garrett-Nordenfelt boat failed because of the loss of the craft, the Russians built two experiemenial 60-ton boats at St. Petersburg in 1899. One was never completed but *Kochka*, the survivor, was forerunner to *Delfin*, an 80ft petrol-driven boat with two torpedoes in slings completed in 1904. Clearly believing in the future of submarines and in a rush of preparation for the Russo-Japanese war, the Russians bought *Protector* from the American Simon Lake. In many ways this was an interesting boat with a separate control room in the bridge, a periscope and a diver's look-out chamber. Despite all this the provision of four retractable wheels showed that Lake had failed to appreciate what he had achieved. Five more were bought, however; *Buichok*, *Kefal*, *Paltus*, *Plotoar* and *Sig. Protector* was renamed *Osetr*.

Delfin

U.S.S.R.

Type: Coastal Submarines (6)
Class: "Holland"
Displacement, tons: 110 surfaced; 120 dived
Dimensions, feet: 63 x 12 x 11
Torpedo armament: 1 x 14in tube (bow)
Main machinery: Petrol engine of 160hp; main motor; 1 shaft
Speed, knots: 9.5 surfaced; 7.5 dived

Complement: 7
Dates: 1905-1908

Notes: This group *(Byeluga, Losos, Peskar, Shuka, Som, Sterlyad)* followed the Lake boats, the first, *Som (ex-Fulton)*, being shaken down for transport from USA and re-assembled at the Nevski Yard where the other five were built.

Byeluga

U.S.S.R.

Type: Coastal Submarines (4)
Class: "Alligator"
Displacement, tons: 450 surfaced; 500 dived
Dimensions, feet: 134 x 15 x 13
Torpedo armament: 4 tubes (2 bow twin external) 2 slings
Guns: 2 x 3 pdr; 2 MG
Main machinery: Petrol engines of 1,200 IHP; 2 main motors; 2 screws.
Speed, knots: 15 surfaced; 7 dived
Complement: 20
Dates: 1909

Notes: This class of Lake boats *(Alligator, Dragon, Kaiman, Krokodil)* was built in Russia, following two interesting classes, the "Kasatka", designed by Professor Bubnov from plans by Captain Beklemiskeff and the German-built "Karp" class. The seven boats, *Delfin* (not to be confused with her immediate predecessor of the same name, the first submarine built in Russia), *Kasatka, Skat, Nalim, Maksel, Graf-Skeremetiev* and *Okun,* of Bubnov's design were of 145 tons dived displacement, propelled by oil engines and of low speed. The "Karp" class followed the unsuccessful *Forel* built by Germaniawerft, Kiel which, although an experimental boat, was the first submarine built in Germany. The "Karps" *(Karp, Karas, Kambala)* were of 240 tons dived displacement with petrol engines and one torpedo tube and built to the designs of the disappointed Frenchman d'Equeville. They were very similar to the U1 built for Germany in the same yard at the same time, though U1 had an oil engine.

Alligator

U.S.S.R.

Type: Patrol Submarines (6)
Class: "Ryss" (later "Bolshevik")
Displacement, tons: 650 surface; 784 dived
Dimensions, feet: 223 x 14.6 x 12.7
Torpedo armament: 4 x 18in tubes. 8 external slings
Guns: 1 x 3in; 1 MG
Main machinery: 2 diesels of 500hp, later 2,500hp; 2 main motors of 900hp; 2 shafts
Speed, knots: 10-16 surfaced; 9 dived
Complement: 30
Dates: 1915-1916

Notes: This class, a Bubnov design; *Ryss* (later *Bolshevik*) *Pantera* (later *Komissar*) *Tigr* (later *Kommunar*), *Yaguar* (later *Krasnoflotetz*) *Leopard* (later *Krasnoarmeyetz*) and *Tier* (later *Tovaritch*), were all built by Nobel and Lessner at Reval. They were the outcome of a number of designs which followed the "Alligator"

class. *Minoga,* launched in 1908, was a Bubnov boat, being notable as the first Russian submarine driven by diesels. Of 177 tons dived displacement she was followed by the larger (400 tons) and more successful *Akula,* a triple-screwed boat which mounted two bow and two stern tubes with four external slings. Meanwhile at Nikolaev Yard the first custom-built submarine minelayer, *Krab,* was laid down. She was seven years building, emerging in 1915 as a 740 ton (dived) submarine with four tubes and carrying 60 mines in the after casing. A different approach was that of B.M. Muravlev who designed a submarine cruiser of 4,500 tons, with a range of 18,000 miles, a speed of 26 knots and carrying 36 torpedo tubes "of an entirely new construction" – 18 on either beam – 120 floating mines and five 120mm guns in armoured turrets. The pressure hull was of ¾in steel with a 2in armoured deck and 3½in vertical armour. Fortunately for Russian submariners this monstrosity got no further than the drawing board. By 1914 Russia had 30 submarines available – those already mentioned plus "Ossetyr" (3) and "Okun" (6) classes.

Bars (Naval Museum, Leningrad)
Ersh (Naval Museum, Leningrad)

U.S.S.R.

Type: Minelaying Submarines (32)
Class: "L"
Displacement, tons: 1,100 surfaced; 1,450 dived
Dimensions, feet: 279 x 23 x 16.5
Torpedo armament: 8 x 21in (6 bow, 2 stern). 12 torpedoes
Mines: 14
Guns: 1 x 4in; 1 x 37mm; 2 MG
Main machinery: 2 diesels of 2,500hp; 2 main motors of 1,200hp; 2 shafts
Speed, knots: 16 surfaced; 9 dived
Complement: 50
Dates: Launched 1929-1935
Special features: Range 7,000 miles at 9 knots surfaced
Notes: Very little is known of the plans for submarine warfare which existed towards the end of the Tsar's regime – the main weight of operations in the Baltic fell on British submarines under Commander Max Horton. In the unsettled period from 1917 onwards the requirement and rôle of the Soviet navy was discussed but little practical action taken. In fact the period 1917-1928 was a period of decline and demoralisation – from then on violent conflict existed between two rival schools of thought which was resolved by Stalin's insistence on a strong ocean-going fleet. One result of this was a submarine building programme which had started with the "L" class (L1-32). Provision and training of personnel must have been a problem as the submarine force had been run-down to less than 20 boats in the 1920's, a mixture of the "Bolshevik" class, some "Holland" boats *(Metallist* etc.) built from 1916-1924, and a group of "one-off" submarines, including British "L" class.

Yakobinetz

U.S.S.R.

Type: Patrol Submarines (7)
Class: "Garibaldietz"
Displacement, tons: 1,039 surfaced; 1,335 dived
Torpedo armament: 6 x 21in
Guns: 1 x 4in; 1 MG
Main machinery: 2 diesels; 2 main motors
Speed, knots: 14 surfaced; 8.5 dived
Complement: 50
Dates: 1933-1935

Notes: With improvements in economic conditions and decisions on the navy's future a major building programme was put in hand. The seven boats of this class *(Garibaldietz, Chartist, Karbonari, Blucher, Budenni, Galler* and *Orlov)* built to an Adriatico design, were the forerunners of a whole flood of submarines which provided the USSR with the largest submarine fleet in the period after World War II.

Garibaldietz

U.S.S.R.

Type: Patrol Submarines (25+?)
Class: "Chuka"
Displacement, tons: 650 surfaced; 748 dived
Torpedo armament: 4 x 21in
Mines: Minelaying capability
Guns: 2 x 1 pdr.
Main machinery: 2 diesels; 2 main motors
Speed, knots: 19 surfaced; 9 dived
Complement: 25
Dates: 1935-1938

Notes: Originally named *Chuka* (301), *Okun* (302), *Ersh* (303), *Makrel* (304), *Sig* (313), *Lin* (305), *Delfin* (309), *Kassatka* (311), *Malim, Osetr, Bitstok, Kesal, Paltus, Plotva, Skat, Som, Losos, Steliad, Forel, Kumsa, Piksta, Semga, Treska, Bieluya, Peskar* +?
All were numbered from 301 when names were dropped.
The "D" class (possibly 6 in all) believed to be a modification of the "Chuka", followed and in 1937 Vickers-Armstrong built the *Lembit*, a minelaying submarine (20 mines) of 820 tons dived displacement, for the Estonian navy. She was subsequently taken over by USSR.

Chuka

U.S.S.R.

Type: Coastal Submarines (283)
Class: "Malutka" (MIV, MV)
Displacement, tons: MIV 205/256; MV 350/420
Dimensions, feet: MIV 147.7 x 11 x 9; MV 167.3 x 16 x 12
Torpedo armament: 2 x 21in tubes
Guns: 1 x 45mm
Main machinery: 2 diesels of 800hp (MIV), 1,000hp (MV); 2 main motors of 400hp (MVI), 800hp (MV); 2 shafts
Speed, knots: 13/8 (MIV); 13/10 (MV)
Complement: 20/24
Dates: 1928-1950 (MI-MV)

Special features: Range MIV-3,400 miles at 8 knots surfaced, 30 hours at 3 knots dived. MV-4000 miles at 10 knots surfaced, 20 hours at 5 knots dived

Notes: The "Malutka" class was an illustration of the result of the "home-defence" complex in the USSR. The figures given above are for the last two groups of this class – the first MI (MI-M76) was started in 1928, was followed by MII (M77) and MIII (M79-101). The MIV variants (102-199) were built during the war and followed by the much larger "MV" class (200-283). A large number were built at Gorki and, being rail-portable in sections, were easily deployed.

Later "M" type

U.S.S.R.

Type: Patrol Submarines (72)
Class: "Shch"
Displacement, tons: 620 surfaced; 738 dived
Dimensions, feet: 190.3 x 19.5 x 13
Torpedo armament: 6 x 21in (20 torpedoes)
Guns: 2 x 45mm; 2 MG
Main machinery: 2 diesels of 1,600bhp; 2 main motors; 2 shafts
Speed, knots: 15.5 surfaced; 8.5 dived
Complement: 40
Dates: 1935-1947 (launched)

Notes: There were several variations of this class during the twelve years they were under construction. Numbered Sh101-141, Sh201, 203, 205, 207, 215, 303, 305, 307-10, 317, 318, Sh400-404, 407, 408, 410-412, 419, 422, 425-431.
The comparatively small size of these boats suggests a "home-defence" role, although British boats of the "U"-class of comparable size achieved patrols of a month or more.

Type: Patrol Submarines (33+)
Class: "S"
Displacement, tons: 780 surfaced; 1,050 dived
Dimensions, feet: 256 x 21 x 13
Torpedo armament: 6 x 21in tubes
Guns: 1 x 3in; 1 x 45mm
Main machinery: 2 diesels of 4,200bhp; 2 main motors of 2,200shp; 2 shafts
Speed, knots: 20 surfaced; 8.5 dived
Complement: 50
Dates: 1937-1940
Special features: Range 9,800 miles at 9 knots surfaced

Notes: This class followed the "P" class *(Pracda* (P1), *Sviezda* (P2) and *Iskra* (P3)) of which few details are available but appears to have been the forerunner of the "K" class.
The number of submarines built to the "S" design is uncertain but at one time pendant numbers ran to S139.

U.S.S.R.

Type: Minelaying Submarines (19+)
Class: "K"
Displacement, tons: 1,457 surfaced; 2,062 dived
Dimensions, feet: 320 x 24 x 14
Torpedo armament: 12 x 21in tubes (6 bow, 4 stern, 2 external, 20 torpedoes)
Mines: 32
Guns: 2 x 4in; 2 x 45mm
Main machinery: 2 diesels of 8,400bhp; 2 main motors of 2,400shp
Speed, knots: 22 surfaced; 10 dived
Complement: 62
Dates: 1939-1943 (launched)
Special features: Range 10,000 miles at 9 knots surfaced

Notes: These were the first large, high-performance submarines built by the USSR except for the "P" class, their immediate predecessors and prototypes. The total number is uncertain but known pendant numbers ranged from K1 to K78.

K-21 (Naval Museum, Leningrad)

U.S.S.R.

Type: Patrol Submarines(22)
Class: "Quebec"
Displacement, knots: 650 surfaced; 740 dived
Dimensions, feet: 185 x 18 x 13.2
Torpedo armament: 4 x 21in tubes (bow)
Main machinery: Diesel 3,000bhp; 3 main motors of 2,500hp; 3 shafts
Speed, knots: 18 surfaced; 16 dived
Complement: 42
Dates: 1954-1957
Special features: See notes

Notes: After World War II the Soviet navy fell into similar disarray to that which followed the 1917 revolution. Several ex-German submarines were taken over and commissioned by the Russians (at least 2 Type IIB, 4 Type VII, 1 Type IXC, 4 Type XXI and 1 Type XXIII). In addition a quantity of hulls and machinery was obtained from German yards, including the Walther turbine with its High Test Peroxide.

The "Quebec" class reflects many of the lessons learned from ex-German acquisitions, chiefly a streamlined hull-form from the Type XXI and a third shaft propelled by a Walther turbine similar to Type XVII/XVIII. Whether the inherent problems of using HTP, a fuel which explodes when in contact with dirt, oil or rust, or the incapacity of crews to operate boats at high speed was the reason is not known but these boats were refitted to standard diesel-electric systems. The majority are now in reserve in the Baltic and Black Seas.

"Quebec" class (Siegfried Breger)

U.S.S.R.

Type: Patrol Submarines(24)
Class: "Whisky"
Displacement, tons: 1,030 surfaced; 1,350 dived
Dimensions, feet: 249.3 x 22 x 15
Torpedo armament: 6 x 21in tubes (4 bow, 2 stern. 18 torpedoes or 40 mines)
Guns: Originally Types I, II and IV had guns. I and IV 1 x 3.9in; 1 x 25mm. Type II 2 x 57mm; 2 x 25mm
Main machinery: Diesel-electric. Diesels of 4,000bhp; 2 main motors of 2,500hp; 2 shafts
Speed, knots: 17 surfaced; 15 dived
Diving depth: 350ft
Complement: 65
Dates: 1951-1957
Special features: Range 13,000 miles at 8 knots surfaced

Notes: The "Whisky" class was the Soviet's first medium-sized post-war submarine. There have been six basic types sighted – I, II and IV with guns (see above) III and V without guns and VA with a diver's exit-hatch before the conning tower. The original design showed strong German influence but subsequent alterations were strictly Russian. The "Twin-Cylinder" was a 1958-1960 conversion fitted with two cylinders abaft the conning-tower for SS-N-3 missiles (Shaddock) with a 150-250 mile range. The "Twin Cylinder's" successor the "Long-Bin" was a more efficient modification of the "Whisky" class with four SS-N-3 launchers built into a remodelled fin on a hull lengthened by 26ft. These conversions were made in 1962-1963 simultaneously with the "Canvas Bag" (3) conversions in which the fitting of "Boat Sail" radar turned these into radar pickets. Now (1974) being paid off at possibly 15-20 per year. Currently about 110 in existence with up to 50% in reserve.

A popular export model – Albania (4), Bulgaria (2), China (21), Egypt (6), Indonesia (10), N. Korea (4), Poland (4).

"WV" class (Niels Gartig)

U.S.S.R.

Type: Patrol Submarines (44+6)
Class: "Zulu"
Displacement, tons: 1,900 surfaced; 2,200 dived
Dimensions, feet: 259.3 x 23.9 x 19
Torpedo armament: 10 x 21in tubes (6 bow, 4 stern. 24 torpedoes or 40 mines)
Main machinery: 3 diesels of 10,000bhp; 3 main motors of 3,500hp; 3 shafts. Diesel-electric
Speed, knots: 18 surfaced; 15 dived
Complement: 70
Dates: 1951-1955

Special features: Range 20,000 miles surfaced at 10 knots

Notes: The largest of the three immediate post-war designs. There were five types – I-IV were normal patrol submarines but the "Zulu V" was a 1955-1957 conversion, being the first Soviet Ballistic Missile class. Two vertical tubes were fitted in the lengthened fin to take SS-N-4 missiles (Sark) with a range of 300 miles.
Three "Zulu IV" class have been converted for oceanographical research *(Lyra, Orion, Vega)* whilst the last two of the six "Zulu V's" have been disarmed and used for fishery research. In all 50 of this class were built of which 19 were operational in 1975.

"Zulu V" class (A.P.N.)

U.S.S.R.

Type: Patrol Submarines (20)
Class: "Romeo"
Displacement, tons: 1,000 surfaced; 1,600 dived
Dimensions, feet: 249.3 x 24 x 14.5
Torpedo armament: 6 x 21in tubes (bow)
Main machinery: 2 diesels of 4,000bhp; 2 main motors of 4,000hp; 2 shafts
Speed, knots: 17 surfaced; 14 dived

Complement: 65
Dates: 1958-1961

Notes: An improvement on the "Whisky" class design built in 1958-61. Twenty were built, twelve remaining operational in 1975, six having been transferred to Egypt. China had a force of thirty "Romeos" in 1975 with a building rate of six per year. All but one or two of this large group were produced in Chinese shipyards.

"Romeo" class

U.S.S.R.

Type: Patrol Submarines (56)
Class: "Foxtrot"
Displacement, tons: 2,000 surfaced; 2,300 dived
Dimensions, feet: 301.7 x 24.1 x 19.0
Torpedo armament: 10 x 21in tubes (6 bow, 4 stern. 20 torpedoes)
Main machinery: Diesels of 6,000bhp; 3 main motors of 6,000hp; 3 shafts
Speed, knots: 20 surfaced; 15 dived
Complement: 70

Dates: 1958-1967
Special features: Range 20,000 miles at 10 knots surfaced

Notes: A splendid class of diesel-boats, probably one of the two best ever built. The majority were constructed at Sudomekh and Leningrad and have, over recent years, borne the main brunt of Soviet foreign deployments. Four were transferred to India in 1968-1970 with four more in 1973-1975.

"Foxtrot" class

U.S.S.R.

Type: Patrol Submarines (4)
Class: "Bravo"
Displacement, tons: 2,500 surfaced; 2,800 dived
Dimensions, feet: 229.6 × 24.8 × 14.8
Torpedo armament: 6 × 21in (bow)
Main machinery: Diesel-electric
Speed, knots: 16 dived
Dates: 1968-1974

Notes: The purpose of this class of conventional submarines is not clear although the fact that there is one with each fleet reinforces the view that these may be "padded targets" for torpedo and A/S firings.

Type: Patrol Submarines (3+?)
Class: "Tango"
Displacement, tons: 2,000 surfaced; 2,500 dived
Dimensions, feet: 300 × 30 × 16
Main machinery: Diesel-electric
Dates: 1973 onwards

Notes: This completely new class of diesel submarine was first seen in July 1973 – the raised fore-casing and new form of snort exhaust are notable features. Coming five years after the appearance of the "Bravo" the main point of interest is the continuing Soviet concern in this type of submarine.

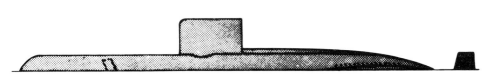

"Bravo" class

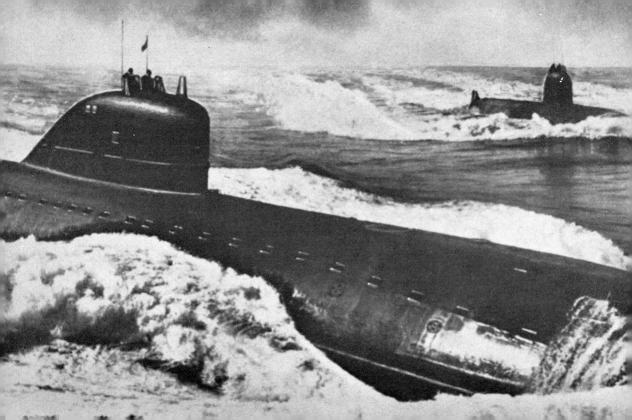

U.S.S.R.

Type: Fleet Submarines (14)
Class: "November"
Displacement, tons: 4,200 surfaced; 4,800 dived
Dimensions, feet: 360.9 x 32.1 x 24.3
Torpedo armament: 6 x 21in (bow)
Main machinery: Nuclear reactor; steam turbines 22,500shp; single screw
Speed, knots: 20 surfaced; 25 dived

Complement: 88
Dates: 1958-1963

Notes: The first class of nuclear propelled submarines in the Soviet Navy. It is hardly surprising that these are noisy boats with their strings of free-flood holes in the casing and early pattern of gearing. In 1970 one of this class foundered in the Atlantic south-west of the U.K.

"November" class

U.S.S.R.

Type: Fleet Submarines (14)
Class: "Victor"
Displacement, tons: 4,400 surfaced; 5,100 dived
Dimensions, feet: 308.3 x 32.8 x 26.2
Torpedo armament: 8 x 21in tubes (bow)
Main machinery: Nuclear reactor; steam turbines 24,000shp; 1 shaft
Speed, knots: 26 surfaced; 30+ dived
Complement: 90?
Dates: 1967 onwards

Notes: This class is a radical advance on the "Novembers". The beam to length ratio has been brought to 8.7 from 11.2 and with very little increase in power the speed has been raised by over 5 knots. At the same time the external hull and casing have been tidied up and these are much quieter submarines. The main surprise is that their building rate is only about two per year. This may have been caused by a desire to carry out trials on the "Alpha" class of which there is only one unit that appeared in 1970. In 1973 the first "Victor II" class was reported, 331ft long and of 6,000 tons dived.

"Victor" class

U.S.S.R.

Type: Cruise-Missile Submarines (16)
Class: "Juliet"
Displacement, tons: 3,200 surfaced; 3,600 dived
Dimensions, feet: 285.4 x 31.4 x 20.0
Missile armament: 4 x SS-N-3 tubes
Torpedo armament: 6 x 21in tubes (bow) 2 or 4 x 16in (stern)
Main machinery: Diesels of 6,000bhp; Main motors of 6,000shp; 2 shafts
Speed, knots: 16 surfaced and dived
Dates: 1962-1967

Special features: Range 15,000 surfaced at 10 knots

Notes: The plans for this class were in hand before the "Whisky Twin Cylinder" class completed its conversion but it is the logical continuation, having four tubes for the "Shaddock" (150-400 mile) missiles and being custom-built for the job. The resultant high casing is unmistakable. This class may be considered something of a "belt and braces" order as it will be seen in the next entry that the nuclear-propelled "Echo I" class pre-dated the "Juliets".

"Juliet" class

U.S.S.R.

Type: Nuclear Cruise-Missile Submarines (5+27)
Class: "Echo" I and II
Displacement, tons: EI 4600/5000; EII 5000/5600
Dimensions, feet: EI 380.9 x 28.4 x 25.9; EII 387.4 x 28.4 x 25.9
Missile armament: EI 6 SS-N-3 launchers; EII 8 SS-N-3 launchers
Torpedo armament: 6 x 21in (bow); 4 x 16in (stern)
Main machinery: Nuclear reactor; steam turbines 22,500shp
Speed, knots: 20 surfaced
Complement: 92/100

Dates: E1 1960-1962; E11 1963-67

Notes: The first of the nuclear propelled submarines with cruise-missiles. In each case the missile tubes are hinged in the casing, the boat having to surface to fire its "Shaddock" missiles. The hull in these classes was even longer and slimmer than in the "Novembers" with a beam to length ratio of 13.6. In 1973-1974 the last of the "Echo I" class was converted to a Fleet Submarine.

"Echo II" class

U.S.S.R.

Type: Nuclear Cruise-Missile Submarines (11)
Class: "Charlie"
Displacement, tons: 4,000 surfaced; 5,100 dived
Dimensions, feet: 304.8 x 32.8 x 24.6
Missile armament: 8 tubes for SS-N-7 missile system
Torpedo armament: 8 x 21in tubes
Main machinery: Nuclear reactor and steam turbines of 24,000shp.
Speed, knots: 20 surfaced; 30+ dived
Complement: 100
Dates: 1968 onwards

Notes: The "Charlie" class was a major advance. With improved hull and machinery design her silence and underwater performance was well ahead of the "Echo" class. But the capacity to launch her eight SS-N-7 missiles (29 mile range) from dived was the really important advance. It must be assumed that the "Charlie" has an organic missile control system and therefore poses a great threat to any force.

A building rate of about 3 a year is being sustained.

A new class "Papa" of which only one unit has been reported, is presumed to be a follow-on to the "Charlie" First announced 1972.

"Charlie" class

U.S.S.R.

Type: Ballistic-Missile Submarines (22)
Class: "Golf" I and II
Displacement, tons: 2,350 surfaced; 2,800 dived
Dimensions, feet: 320 x 25.1 x 22
Missile armament: 3 launchers for SS-N-4 system (SSN-5 II)
Torpedo armament: 10 x 21in tubes (6 bow, 4 stern)
Main machinery: 3 diesels of 6,000bhp; 2 main motors of 6,000shp; 3 shafts
Speed, knots: 17.6 surfaced; 17 dived

Complement: 86
Dates: 1959-1962
Special features: Range 22,700 miles surfaced at 10 knots

Notes: This class, built largely at Severodvinsk and Komsomolsk, started life (GI) with SS-N-4 system with "Sark" (300 mile range) missiles. Half of the class was converted to the SS-N-5 system with 700 mile "Serb" missiles (GII). This was the last diesel-driven ballistic missile submarine yet built.

"Golf 1" class

U.S.S.R.

Type: Nuclear Ballistic Missile Submarines (10)
Class: "Hotel" I and II
Displacement, tons: 3,700 surfaced; 4,100 dived
Dimensions, feet: 377.2 x 28.2 x 25
Missile armament: 3 launchers for SS-N-5 (originally SS-N-4) missiles
Torpedo armament: 6 x 21in tubes (bow) 4 x 16in. (stern)
Main machinery: Nuclear reactor – steam turbines, 22,500shp; 1 shaft
Speed, knots: 20 dived

Complement: 90
Dates: 1958-1962

Notes: This class was an advance as it was the first nuclear-propelled ballistic missile submarine in the Soviet Navy. The "Hotel I" class carried "Sark" (300 mile) missiles for the SS-N-4 system. Subsequent refit provided the SS-N-5 system ("Hotel II") with the 700 mile "Serb" missiles. One of this class, designated "Hotel III" was transformed to fire the SSNX-8 missile, the prototype of the missiles carried by the later "Delta" class.

"Hotel" class

U.S.S.R.

Type: Nuclear Ballistic Missile Submarines (33)
Class: "Yankee"
Displacement, tons: 8,000 surfaced; 9,000 dived
Dimensions, feet: 426.5 x 34.8 x 32.8
Missile armament: 16 launchers for SS-N-6 system
Torpedo armament: 8 x 21in tubes
Main machinery: Nuclear reactor; steam turbines, 24,000shp
Speed, knots: 20 surfaced; 25 dived
Complement: 120
Dates: 1968-1972

Notes: The Soviets are never far behind and the "Yankee" class was, in 1968, the expected riposte to Polaris. The weapon itself, the "Sawfly" missile for the SS-N-6 system, was not, however, of comparable performance to Polaris. Its range of 1,300 miles allowed well-placed submarines to cover the majority of Europe as well as most of Canada and the USA. But it did require these boats to encroach well in towards the target coastlines and this was clearly unsatisfactory. Details of the American long-range SOSUS system had been bandied about by scientists at Venice – the Soviets needed to withdraw into more friendly waters. By the end of 1972 the method was displayed in the "Delta" class.

"Yankee" class

U.S.S.R.

Type: Nuclear Ballistic Missile Submarines (19+2)
Class: "Delta" and "Delta II"
Displacement, tons: 8,500 surfaced; 10,000 dived
Dimensions, feet: 450 x 34.8 x 32.8
Missile armament: 12 launchers for SS-N-8 system
Torpedo armament: 8 x 21in tubes
Main machinery: Nuclear reactors; steam turbines; 2 screws
Speed, knots: 20 surfaced; 25 dived
Complement: 120 approx.
Dates: 1972 onwards

Notes: All details above are for "Delta" class, which was the largest submarine so far built. So large in fact that two screws are included. The SS-N-8 system fires a missile of 4,200 miles range, capable of striking throughout North America and Europe without the parent boat passing the Greenland-Iceland-Faroes Gap and thus well-insulated from SOSUS (see previous entry).

This deadly monster, however, did not long retain her title. In November 1973 an even bigger submarine "Delta II" was reported. Of 16,000 tons and possibly carrying 16 missiles the "Delta II"s have outrun the USN "Trident" programme by at least six years.

"Delta" class

Delfino (Italian Navy)

Glauco (Italian Navy)

ITALY

Type: Coastal Submarines (5)
Class: "Glauco"
Displacement, tons: 150 surfaced; 215 dived
Dimensions, feet: 118 x 10 x 14.5
Torpedo armament: 2 tubes (3 in *Glauco*)
Main machinery: 1-4 cylinder petrol engine of 600IHP; 1 main motor; 1 shaft
Speed, knots: 14 surfaced; 7 dived
Complement: 12 (?)
Dates: 1906-1910

Special features: Range 500 miles at 10 knots surfaced

Notes: In 1890 the Italian Navy leaped into the submarine field with *Delfino*, a 100 ton boat designed by Pulino with a surface speed of 9 knots, and mounting one torpedo tube. Equally smartly the Italians leaped out until, in 1905, the first of the "Glauco" class (*Glauco, Tricheco, Narvalo, Otaria,* and *Squalo*) was laid down. These were larger boats and in 1908 the *Foca*, of very similar dimensions to the *Glauco*, was launched.

ITALY

Type: Coastal Submarines (8)
Class: "Argo"
Displacement, tons: 300 surfaced; 345 dived
Torpedo armament: 2 tubes
Main machinery: Diesel engine of 600hp; main motor
Speed, knots: 13 surfaced; 8.5 dived
Complement: 14
Dates: 1911-1912 (launched)
Special features: Range 1,200 miles at 9 knots surfaced

Notes: Nearly twice as large as *Foca* this class (*Argo, Fisalia, Falea, Medusa, Salpa, Santina, Velella, Zoea*) was all launched in 1911-1912. Equipped with a diesel engine this was a considerable improvement on previous designs.
At about the same time three other designs were built, "Nautilus" (*Nautilus, Nereide*) to Bernardi's plans and slightly smaller than "Argo", *Atropo* (a German design with heavy-oil engine) and "G Pullino" (*G Pullino, G Ferraris*) somewhat larger than "Argo" and designed by Cavallini.

Argo (Commander Aldo Fraccaroli)
Galileo Ferraris (Italian Navy)

ITALY

Type: Coastal Submarines (21)
Class: "Fiat-Laurenti"
Displacement, tons: 260 surfaced; 318 dived
Dimensions, feet: 149.5 x 13.7 x 10.3
Torpedo armament: 2 x 17.7in tubes
Guns: 1 x 14pdr
Main machinery: 2 Fiat diesels of 700bhp; 2 main motors of 320hp; 2 shafts
Speed, knots: 13.5 surfaced; 7.5 dived

Complement: 22
Dates: 1916-1917
Special features: Range 1,100 miles at 9 knots surfaced, 70 hours at 1.5 knots dived

Notes: F1-21 built at La Spezia and Livorno. These boats bore a strange resemblance to the much later German Type XXIII in appearance.

"F6"

ITALY

Type: Patrol Submarines (8)
Class: "Holland"
Displacement, tons: 316 surfaced; 441 dived
Dimensions, feet: 150.3 x 15.7 x 12.3
Torpedo armament: 4 x 18in tubes (bow)
Guns: 1 x 14pdr
Main machinery: 2 diesels of 960hp; 2 main motors of 680hp; 2 shafts
Speed, knots: 12.6 surfaced; 11 dived

Notes: H1-8 built by Canadian Vickers, Montreal, bringing Italy into line with many other navies using the "Holland" design. The most notable feature here was the underwater speed, a shade more than the British "H" boats. H5 was sunk during the war.

Complement: 22
Dates: 1917
Special features: Range 2,000 miles at 7.5 knots surfaced, 65 hours at 2 knots dived

"H1"

ITALY

Type: Patrol submarines (6)
Class: "N"
Displacement, tons: 276 surfaced; 357 dived
Dimensions, feet: 151 x 14.7 x 10
Torpedo armament: 2 x 18in tubes (bow)
Guns: 1 x 4pdr
Main machinery: 2 diesels of 720hp; 2 main motors of 330hp; 2 shafts
Speed, knots: 13.6 surfaced; 8 dived
Complement: 21
Dates: 1917-1918
Special features: Range 1,300 miles at 10 knots surfaced, 80 hours at 2.5 knots dived

Notes: Built to Bernardi's design this class (N1-6) was built by Ansaldo, La Spezia and Tosi, Taranto. Although slightly later than the "H" boats their smaller size gave an inferior dived performance.

"N"3 (Italian Navy)

ITALY

Type: Patrol Submarines (4)
Class: "Agostino Barbarigo"
Displacement, tons: 747 surfaced; 925 dived
Dimensions, feet: 213.3 x 19.7 x 13.3
Torpedo armament: 6 x 17.7in tubes
Guns: 2 x 14pdr
Main machinery: 2 diesels of 2,600hp; 2 main motors of 1,100hp
Speed, knots: 17 surfaced; 9.2 dived
Dates: 1917-1918

Special features: Range 1,500 miles at 11.5 knots surfaced, 16 hours at 6 knots dived

Notes: Built by Fiat-San Giorgio La Spezia these boats (*Agostino Barbarigo, Andrea Provana, Sebastiano, Veniero, Giacomo Nani*) were powerful and efficient submarines with the one exception of surface range. The latter however, reflects the expectation of operations in the vicinity of home ports in the Mediterranean.

Agostino Barbarigo (Italian Navy)

ITALY

Type: Patrol Submarines (6)
Class: "Pietro Micca"
Displacement, tons: 840 surfaced; 1,005 dived
Dimensions, tons: 206.7 x 19.5 x 14
Torpedo armament: 6 x 17.7in tubes
Guns: 2 x 14pdr
Main machinery: 2 diesels of 2,600bhp; 2 main motors; 2 shafts
Speed, knots: 15 surfaced; 9.5 dived
Dates: 1914-1919 (see notes)
Special features: Range 1,900 miles at 10 knots, surfaced, 75 hours at 3.5 knots dived

Notes: Built to a Cavallini design this class (*Angelo Emo, Lorenzo Marcello, Lazzaro Mocenigo, Luigi Galvani, Pietro Micca, Evangelista Torricelli*) showed improved surface range over the "Barbarigo" class. The first three named submarines were begun at Venice in August 1914. In the summer of 1915 with the war on the Austrian frontier looking sinister, they were dismantled and taken to La Spezia where they were laid down again. Their completion was thus delayed until 1918-1919.

Pietro Micca (Italian Navy)

ITALY

Type: Patrol Submarines (4+3)
Class: "Balilla"
Displacement, tons: 1,368 surfaced; 1,874 dived
Dimensions, feet: 282 x 24.5 x 14
Torpedo armament: 6 x 21in tubes (4 bow, 2 stern)
Guns: 1 x 4.7in; 4 x 13mm (2 x 4.7in in later boats)
Main machinery: 2 diesels of 4,400bhp; 2 main motors of 2,200bhp; 2 shafts
Speed, knots: 17.5 surfaced; 9.5 dived
Diving depth: 400ft
Complement: 64
Dates: 1927-1928
Special features: 140 tons of oil fuel. Range 13,000 miles at 9 knots surfaced, 20 hours at 4 knots dived

Notes: This class (*Balilla, Antonio Sciesa, Enrico Toti, Dominico Millelite*) built to an Odero design was of exceptionally strong construction achieving an unprecendented safe diving depth. The main machinery was placed further forward than before, bow hydroplanes were not fitted and alterations were made to the distribution of ballast tanks.

The "Calvi" class (*Pietro Calvi, Enrico Tazzoli* and *Giuseppi Finzi*), was an improvement on the "Balilla" laid down in 1932. The main changes were the addition of two extra tubes and another 4.7in gun.

Balilla (Italian Navy)

ITALY

Type: Patrol Submarines (4)
Class: "Mameli"
Displacement, tons: 770 surfaced; 994 dived
Dimensions, feet: 213.3 x 21.3 x 13
Torpedo armament: 6 x 21in tubes
Guns: 1 x 4in; 2 x 13mm
Main machinery: 2 diesels of 3,000bhp; 2 main motors of 1,100bhp; 2 shafts
Speed, knots: 17 surfaced; 9 dived

Diving depth: 330ft
Complement: 46
Dates: 1927-1929

Notes: These Cavallini designed submarines (*Goffredo Mameli, Pier Capponi, Tito Speri, Giovanni da Proccida*) were built in Taranto. Their construction was clearly robust as *Mameli* herself reached a depth of 385ft on trials.

Mameli (Italian Navy)

ITALY

Type: Minelaying Submarines (2)
Class: "Corridoni"
Displacement, tons: 803 surfaced; 1,051 dived
Dimensions, feet: 234.5 x 20 x 13.5
Torpedo armament: 4 x 21in tubes
Mines: 2 chutes, 24 mines
Guns: 1 x 4in; 2 MG
Main machinery: 2 diesels of 1,500hp; 2 main motors of 1,000hp; 2 shafts
Speed, knots: 14 surfaced; 8 dived
Complement: 47
Dates: 1930-1931

Notes: This class (*Marcantonio Bragadino* and *Filippo Corridoni*) were built at Taranto.
The only previous minelayers built for the Italian Navy were the small (453 tons dived) "X" class (X1-3) built by Ansaldo in 1916. They carried 18 mines.

Corridoni (Bargini)

ITALY

Type: Patrol Submarines (4)
Class: "Pisani"
Displacement, tons: 791 surfaced; 1,040 dived
Dimensions, feet: 223 x 19 x 14
Torpedo armament: 6 x 21in tubes
Guns: 1 x 4in; 2 x 13mm
Main machinery: 2 diesels of 2,700hp; 2 main motors of 1,200hp; 2 shafts
Speed, knots: 17.5 surfaced; 9 dived

Complement: 46
Dates: 1928-1929

Notes: This Bernardi's design (*Vittorio Pisani, Giovanni Bausan, Marcantonio Colonna, Ammiraglio Des Geneys*) were all built at Monfalcone. They were the forerunners of a series of classes of submarines in a rapidly expanding navy designed to ensure Mussolini's hold on 'Mare Nostrum'.

Vittorio Pisani (Italian Navy)

ITALY

Type: Patrol Submarines (4+4)
Class: "Squalo" "Santarosa"
Displacement, tons: 810 surfaced; 1,077 dived
Dimensions, feet: 229 x 18.7 x 16.3
Torpedo armament: 8 x 21in tubes
Guns: 1 x 4in; 2 x 13mm
Main machinery: 2 diesels of 3,000hp; 2 main motors of 1,400hp; 2 shafts
Speed, knots: 16.5 surfaced; 9 dived

Diving depth: 350ft
Complement: 48
Dates: 1931

Notes: This class (*Delfino, Narvalo, Squalo* and *Trichecho*) and their predecessors of the "Santarosa" class (*Santorre, Santarosa, Ciro Menotti, Fratelli Bandiera* and *Luciano Manara*) were all of Bernardi's design being improvements on the "Pisani" class. Details above are for "Squalo" class.

Squalo (Italian Navy)

ITALY

Type: Patrol Submarines (2)
Class: "Settembrini"
Displacement, tons: 798 surfaced; 1,134 dived
Dimensions, feet: 226.7 x 25.3 x 11.3
Torpedo armament: 8 x 21in
Guns: 1 x 4in; 2 x 13mm
Main machinery: 2 diesels of 2,000hp; 2 main motors of 1,400hp; 2 shafts
Speed, knots: 17.5 surfaced; 9 dived
Complement: 48
Dates: 1931-1932
Special features: Range 9,000 miles at 8 knots surfaced

Notes: A Cavallini design (*Luigi Settembrini* and *Ruggiero Settimo*) built at Taranto.

Settembrini (Italian Navy)

ITALY

Type: Patrol Submarines (12+7)
Class: "Sirena". "Argonauta"
Displacement, tons: 590 surfaced; 787 dived
Dimensions, feet: 197.5 x 21 x 12
Torpedo armament: 6 x 21in tubes (12 torpedoes)
Guns: 1 x 3.9in; 2/4 x 13mm
Main machinery: 2 diesels of 1,200hp; 2 main motors of 800hp; 2 shafts
Speed, knots: 14 knots surfaced; 8 dived

Complement: 45
Dates: 1933-1934

Notes: This class (*Ametista, Anfitrite, Diamante, Galatea, Naiade, Nereide, Ondina, Rubino, Sirena, Smeraldo, Topazio* and *Zaffiro*) and their predecessors of the "Argonauta" class (*Argonauta, Fisalia, Jalea, Jantina, Medusa, Salpa* and *Serpente*) were all of Bernardi's design.

Sirena (Italian Navy)

ITALY

Type: Patrol Submarines (10)
Class: "Perla"
Displacement, tons: 620 surfaced; 853 dived
Dimensions feet: 197.5 x 21 x 13
Torpedo armament: 6 x 21in tubes (12 torpedoes)
Guns: 1 x 3.9in; 2/4 x 13mm
Main machinery: 2 diesels of 1,400hp; 2 main motors of 800hp; 2 shafts
Speed, knots: 14 surfaced; 8 dived
Diving depth: 300ft

Complement: 45
Dates: 1936

Notes: Very similar to "Sirena" class (*Ambra, Berillo, Corallo, Diaspro, Gemma, Iride, Malachite, Onice, Perla* and *Turchese*). *Iride* and *Onice* served with the Spanish Nationalist Forces in 1937 as *Lopez* and *Tablada* with their own ships' companies. *Perla* was captured at sea in 1942 and became the Greek *Matrozos*. See notes under "Brin" class for similar submarines.

Perla

ITALY

Type: Patrol Submarines (4)
Class: "Archimede"
Displacement, tons: 985 surfaced; 1,259 dived
Dimensions, feet: 231.3 x 22.5 x 13
Torpedo armament: 8 x 21in tubes (16 torpedoes)
Guns: 2 x 3.9in; 2 x 13mm
Main machinery: 2 diesels of 3,000hp; 2 main motors of 1,300hp; 2 shafts
Speed, knots: 17 surfaced; 8.5 dived
Complement: 55

Dates: 1934-1935

Notes: This Cavallini designed class (*Galileo Ferraris, Galileo Galilei, Evangelista Torricelli* and *Archimede*) was very similar to the ex-Portuguese "Glauco" class (*Glauco* and *Otaria*). The last two of the "Archimede" class were transferred to the Spanish Navy in 1937 as *San Vurjo* and *Mola*. *Galilei* was captured in the Red Sea in 1940 by HMS *Moonstone*, subsequently becoming HMS *P711*. Shortly before this time the *Ettore Fieramosca* of 2,128 tons dived had been built but no futher similar boats were produced.

Archimede (Italian Navy)

ITALY

Type: Minelaying Submarines (3)
Class: "Foca"
Displacement, tons: 1,109 surfaced; 1,533 dived
Dimensions, feet: 266.7 x 23.5 x 12.5
Torpedo armament: 6 x 21in tubes
Mines: 2 chutes for 36 mines
Guns: 1 x 3.9in; 4 x 13mm
Main machinery: 2 diesels of 2,880hp; 2 main motors of 1,250hp; 2 shafts

Speed, knots: 16 surfaced; 8 dived
Diving depth: 350ft
Complement: 60
Dates: 1937-1939

Notes: These (*Foca, Zoea, Atropo*) were slightly smaller editions of Cavallini's 1935 design for a minelayer, *Pietro Micca*. (1883 tons dived).

Foca (Italian Navy)

ITALY

Type: Patrol Submarines (3)
Class: "Calvi"
Displacement, tons: 1,550 surfaced; 2,060 dived
Dimensions, feet: 276.5 x 25.5 x 13
Torpedoe armament: 8 x 21in tubes (16 torpedoes)
Guns: 2 x 4.7in; 4 x 13mm
Main machinery: 2 diesels of 4,400hp; 2 main motors of 1,800hp; 2 shafts
Speed, knots: 17 surfaced; 8 dived
Diving depth: 330ft
Complement: 77
Dates: 1935-1936
Special features: Range 13,500 miles at 9 knots surfaced; 20 hours at 4 knots dived

Notes: This class (*Pietro Calvi, Giuseppe Finzi* and *Enrico Tazzoli*) was an improvement of the "Balilla" class. The last pair was converted for use as transport submarines to and from Japan.

Pierro Calvi (Italian Navy)

ITALY

Type: Patrol Submarines (5)
Class: "Brin"
Displacement, tons: 1,016 surfaced; 1,266 dived
Dimensions, feet: 231.3 x 22.5 x 13.5
Torpedo armament: 8 x 21in tubes (14 torpedoes)
Guns: 1 x 3.9in; 2 x 13mm
Main machinery: 2 diesels of 3,400hp; 2 main motors of 1,300hp; 2 shafts
Speed, knots: 17 surfaced; 9 dived
Diving depth: 360ft
Complement: 58
Dates: 1938-1939

Notes: There were originally three boats in this class (*Brin*, *Galvani* and *Guglielmotti*) but two extra, *Archimede* and *Torricelli*, were secretly constructed to replace their namesakes transferred to Spain.

Subsequently the "Liuzzi" class of five boats, the "Marconi" class of six boats, the "Cagni" class of four boats, the "Remo" class of which only two transport submarines out of twelve were completed, provided the main bulk of the Italian war-time programmes of larger submarines. The immediate pre-war and war-time programmes of smaller submarines consisted of the 850 ton "Adua" class of 17 boats, very similar to the "Perla" class, the 1,000 ton "Argo" class of three boats, the 13 boats of the "Acciaio" class, again similar to the "Perlas" and the eight boats completed out of the 27 laid down of the 1,131 ton "Flutto" class. The majority of the last of these were captured on the slips by the retreating Germans in 1943 most being broken up.

Brin (Italian Navy)

ITALY

Type: Patrol Submarines (4)
Class: "Toti"
Displacement, tons: 524 surfaced; 582 dived
Dimensions, feet: 151.5 x 15.4 x 13.1
Torpedo armament: 4 x 21in tubes
Main machinery: 2 Fiat diesels; 1 main motor of 2,200hp diesel-electric; 1 shaft
Speed, knots: 14 surfaced; 15 dived
Complement: 31
Dates: 1968-1969
Special features: Range 3,000 miles at 5 knots surfaced

Notes: These four boats (*Attilio Bagnolini, Enrico Dandolo, Lazzaro Mocenigo, Enrico Toti*) were the first built in Italy (by C.R.D.A. Monfalcone) since World War II. Although small in size they have a full set of passive/active sonar with passive range-finding and a ray-path analyser. In addition they mount search radar, I.F.F., E.C.M. and use computerised fire-control.
In 1967 a follow-on class, the "Sauro" class was ordered but cancelled in 1968, being re-instated four years later. Two boats of this class are currently (1975) building being of 1,450 tons dived displacement, mounting six 21in bow tubes and, with a single shaft, capable of 19 knots dived.

Toti (Dr. Georgio Arra)

INDEX

A (UK)	70,98
A1, A2 (Japan)	173
Adder (USA)	12
Agosta (France)	153
Agastino Barbarigo (Italy)	223
Albacore (USA)	45
Alligator (USA)	191
AM (Japan)	173
Amarante (France)	137
Archimede (Italy)	233
Arethuse (France)	151
Argo (USSR)	219
Argonaut (USA)	31
Argonauta (Italy)	231
Ariane (France)	140
B (UK)	71
B1, B2, B3 (Japan)	174
Balao (USA)	42
Balilla (Italy)	225
Barbel (USA)	47
Barracuda (USA)	30
Bellone (France)	137
Bolshevik (USSR)	193
Bravo (USSR)	205
Brin (Italy)	236
C (UK)	72
C1, C2, C3 (Japan)	175
Cachalot (USA)	34
Calvi (Italy)	235
Charlie (USSR)	211
Chuka (USSR)	196
Churchill (UK)	101
Corridoni (Italy)	227
Cuttlefish (USA)	13

D (UK)	73
D1, D2 (Japan)	177
Daphne (France)	152
Delta I & II (USSR)	215
Diane (France)	141
Dolphin (USA)	33
Dreadnought (UK)	100
Dupuy de Lome (France)	138
E (UK)	75
Early Russian (Protector) (USSR)	187
Echo I & II (USSR)	210
Ethan Allen (USA)	65
F (UK)	77
F1, F2 (Japan)	161
Fiat-Laurenti (Italy)	220
Foca (Italy)	234
Foxtrot (USSR)	204
G (UK)	78
G1-3 (USA)	17
G4 (USA)	18
Gar (USA)	39
Garibaldietz (USSR)	195
Gato (USA)	41
George Washington (USA)	63
Glauco (USSR)	217
Golf I & II (USSR)	212
Gustave Zedé (France)	131,136
H (UK)	79
H1-3 (USA)	19
Hayashio (Japan)	157
Holland (Italy)	221
Holland (Japan)	157
Holland (UK)	69

INDEX

Holland (USSR)	189
Hotel I & II (USSR)	213
J (UK)	80
J1, J2 (Japan)	169
J3 (Japan)	173
JM (Japan)	169
Joessel (France)	139
Juliet (USSR)	209
K (UK)	82
K (USSR)	199
K1-8 (USA)	20
K1, K2 (Japan)	163
K3, K4 (Japan)	165
K5, K6 (Japan)	172
KD1, KD2 (Japan)	166
KD3, KD4, KD5, KD6, KD7 (Japan)	171
KRS (Japan)	170
KS (Japan)	176
KT (Japan)	168
L (UK)	83
L (USSR)	194
L1-4 (USA)	21
L5-8 (USA)	22
L9-11 (USA)	21
L1, L2, L3 (Japan)	164
L4 (Japan)	167
Lafayette (USA)	67
La Grange (France)	138
L'Aurore (France)	149
Le Redoubtable (France)	155
Los Angeles (USA)	62
M (UK)	84
M1 (USA)	23
Malutka (USSR)	197
Mameli (Italy)	226
N (Italy)	222
N1 (USA)	24
N4-7 (USA,	25
Narval (France)	133,150
Narwhal (USA)	15,32,61
Nautilus (USA)	49
November (USA)	207
O (UK)	87
O1-10 (USA)	27
Oberon (UK)	99
Octopus (USA)	14
Ooshio (Japan)	183
Oyashio (Japan)	182
P (UK)	88
Perch (USA)	35
Perla (Italy)	232
Permit (ex-Thresher) (USA)	57
Pietro Micca (Italy)	224
Pike (USA)	35
Pisani (Italy)	228
Pluvôise (France)	135
Porpoise (UK)	94,99
Quebec (USSR)	200
R (UK)	85,89
R1-27 (USA)	28
Redoubtable-1500 tonne (France)	145
Requin (France)	142
Resolution (UK)	102
Romeo (USSR)	203

INDEX

Ryss (USSR) ... 193

S (UK) ... 93
S/S2 (Japan) ... 159
S1-S51 (USA) ... 29
Salmon (USA) ... 37
Santarosa (Italy) ... 229
Saphir (France) ... 143
Sargo (USA) ... 38
Settembrini (Italy) ... 230
SH (Japan) ... 178
Shch (USSR) ... 198
Sirena (Italy) ... 231
Skate (USA) ... 50
Skipjack (USA) ... 16,51
Squalo (Italy) ... 229
ST (Japan) ... 180
STO (Japan) ... 179
STS (Japan) ... 181
Sturgeon (USA) ... 59
Surcouf (France) ... 147
Swiftsure (UK) ... 101

T (UK) ... 97
Tambor (USA) ... 39
Tang (USA) ... 44
Tench (USA) ... 43
Thames (UK) ... 90
Toti (Italy) ... 237
Triton (USA) ... 53
Tulibee (USA) ... 55

U1, 2, 3, 5 (Germany) ... 103
U9, 13, 16, 17 (Germany) ... 104
U19, 23, 27, 31, 43, 51 (Germany) ... 105

U57, 60, 63, 66 (Germany) ... 106
U71, 73, 75 (Germany) ... 107
U81 (Germany) ... 108
U87 (Germany) ... 109
U93, 96 (Germany) ... 110
U99 (Germany) ... 111
U105, 111 (Germany) ... 112
U117, 122 (Germany) ... 113
U135 (Germany) ... 114
U139, 142 (Germany) ... 115
U151 (Germany) ... 116
U160 (Germany) ... 117
UB (Germany) ... 118
UC (Germany) ... 119
IA, IIA, IIB, IIC, IID (Germany) ... 120
VIIA, VIIB, VIIC (Germany) ... 121
VIID, VIIF (Germany) ... 122
IXA, IXB, IXC, IXC 40, IXD (Germany) ... 123
XB, XI (Germany) ... 124
XIV (Germany) ... 125
XVIIA, XVIIB (Germany) ... 126
XXI (Germany) ... 127
XXIII (Germany) ... 128
201, 205, 206 (Germany) ... 129

V (UK) ... 76
Valiant (UK) ... 101
Vickers C1, C2 (Japan) ... 158
Victor (USSR) ... 208

Whisky (USSR) ... 201

X1 (UK) ... 86

Yankee (USSR) ... 214

Zulu (USSR) ... 202